Getting Custody

Robert Henley Woody, Ph.D., Sc.D.
Diplomate in Clinical Psychology, A.B.P.P.

Getting Custody

Winning the Last Battle of the Marital War

Macmillan Publishing Co., Inc.
NEW YORK

Macmillan Publishing Co., Inc.
866 Third Avenue, New York, N.Y. 10022
Collier Macmillan Canada, Ltd.

Library of Congress Cataloging in Publication Data

Woody, Robert Henley.
Getting custody.

Bibliography: p.
Includes index.
1. Custody of children—United States. I. Title.
KF547.W66 346'.73'017 77-28693
ISBN 0-02-631570-X

First Printing 1978

Designed by Jack Meserole

Printed in the United States of America

Dedicated to
my wife,
JANE DIVITA WOODY,
and our children,
JENNIFER, BOBBY,
and MATTHEW

Contents

PREFACE, ix

1. With You as a Friend, Who Needs an Enemy? 1

2. I'll Keep the Car, You Keep the Kids, 14

3. Power to the Children, 21

4. Old War Wounds (And a Few New Ones, Too), 29

5. The Cease-Fire Line, 44

6. The Gladiators: The Mamas and the Papas, 57

7. The Battle Plan, 68

8. Choosing Your Weapons, 90

9. Being Prepared: Strategy, Not Fury, 111

10. Recruiting Allies, 135

11. The Reconstruction Period, 157

APPENDIX A Top Twenty Factors for Mothers, 168

APPENDIX B Top Twenty Factors for Fathers, 169

About the Author, 170

REFERENCES, 172

INDEX, 174

Preface

It is widely acknowledged that divorce has reached "epidemic" proportions in contemporary American society. The increase in divorce brings with it an increase in the number of children affected by the absence of one parent from day-to-day contact with the child. Consequently, state child-custody statutes are now reflecting a new thrust: *the concept of the best interests of the child.* That is, it is recognized that divorce creates a special problem for children and that custody decisions should be based on consideration of the welfare of the children.

Concurrently, equal-rights laws have been interpreted as extending into child-custody determinations. No longer is the mother automatically given custody of the children. The father has a right to equal consideration, with the major determinant being, as mentioned, which parent can best fulfill the needs of the children.

Parents who have divorced (or are contemplating divorce) usually know little, if anything, about the criteria for child-custody determinations. The standard approach is to hire an attorney and wait until the court takes action. Such passive dependence is not in the best interests of either parents or children. There must be responsible involvement in the child-custody proceedings.

Having worked as a psychotherapist and marriage and family counselor and having conducted research on the evaluation processes for child-custody determinations, I have brought together information on the history and status of child custody in America, the legal factors prescribed by state child-custody statutes, and the criteria that will be applied in evaluating whether you or your ex-spouse should be awarded custody. Regarding the last topic, much of my research has focused upon professionals who can be brought into the custody proceedings to evaluate parents' ability for fulfilling the best interests of the child. These professionals include lawyers, psychiatrists, psychologists, social workers, and others. Herein, I offer you a practical explanation of what these research findings support, such as how different types of professionals view the criteria to be applied to you (and their views do differ according to their personal characteristics and disciplines and according to whether they are being applied to a mother or a father) and how you can select professionals to contribute to your efforts to win custody. Being a psychotherapist, I am aware of the psychological impact of divorce and custody decisions, and I present ideas gleaned from working with hundreds of therapy clients about coping with the pressures and, of most importance, maintaining the strength to be a good parent and to find a new rewarding life after the dust has settled from the divorce and custody proceedings.

Preface

In approaching the issue of child custody, I want to emphasize that there is the implicit question: Should you seek custody? As will be brought out in this book, society has conditioned most of us into believing that a mother should have custody and that a father is not able to care for the children. In point of fact, there are some mothers who do not want and/or should not have custody, while there are others who want and should receive it. Conversely, some fathers are unquestionably better able to care for the children than some mothers. Neither the mother nor the father should assume that gender preordains who should receive custody.

Getting custody requires of the parent a strong commitment to the child and a strong sense of responsibility. Self-responsibility is difficult enough, but parenting—especially single parenting—goes even further because the welfare and existence of another person are dependent upon your actions.

Pursuit of custody mandates that the parent, be it the mother or father, be prepared to make the welfare of the children primary in life. Certainly there can, should, and must be maintenance of a personal life by the parent, such as having friends and social activities, but in all realms, adult needs have to be balanced with parental responsibility.

Failing to get custody does not brand a parent as "no good," nor does it remove continued responsibility to the children. Granted, there is a redefinition of parental involvement, but the healthy strategy for the parent without custody is to strive to provide the children with caring and positive influence throughout life.

Given the foregoing, I believe that the contents of this book should help you understand the manner in which child-custody determinations are made, the criteria used to evaluate parents, and the professionals who can aid you in a custody dispute.

On a more personal level, you should get important therapeutic ideas as to how you can, if involved in child-custody situations, cope effectively with the real problems that will ensue and the emotional and behavioral considerations for both you and your children. From these ideas, you can plan ways to reorganize your life so that you can both meet the best interests of the children and develop a route to improved living and happiness.

Special emphasis will be given to how you can map a strategy for winning a battle for custody. Throughout the book there will be discussion of the responsibilities of getting custody, so that you should complete the book with a better understanding of whether you do or do not wish to enter into a custody contest.

ROBERT HENLEY WOODY, PH.D., SC.D.
Diplomate in Clinical Psychology, A.B.P.P.

Getting Custody

1.

With You as a Friend, Who Needs an Enemy?

THE AMERICAN FAMILY of today is vastly different from that of the past—even the recent past. And the difference is much more than simply an adult's idealizing the past. Conditions for living—the political scene, the economy, morals, and values—create a new perspective for establishing and maintaining a marriage and a family.

Children, because of their dependence upon adults, face special problems as a result of these changing and new conditions. When adults are placed under stress (such as from unemployment or divorce), there are reactions within the entire family. First, the adults have *covert* responses, such as feeling insecure or frustrated. And second, they have *overt* responses, such as turning the frustration and disappointment into anger toward their spouses or rejection and neglect of their children. Chapter 4 will discuss this matter further.

Improving a marriage and controlling family problems are subjects that have received much attention. Some of my views can be found in my book *Sexual, Marital, and Familial Relations* (Woody & Woody, 1972). Indeed, probably no other aspect of human behavior has been explored so extensively through research and in books, scholarly journals, and magazines in the last five years. Still, marriage and family problems continue to perplex professionals and lay persons alike.

On the other hand, the effects of the marriage for the children have received scant attention. In fact, children have long been deprived of consideration in professional dealings with the family. This is particularly evident in the fact that children have not had legal representation in child-custody legal proceedings. If the custody is contested, the mother has a lawyer representing her interests and the father has a lawyer representing his interests, but the children are left to be fitted into the interests of whichever parent is declared by the court to be the more fit.

In a moment we will move into the matter of children's rights and child custody and how you, as a parent, can find personal fulfillment by adopting a new perspective of child custody—and, in the process, gaining custody of your children, should you be faced with such a quest. But first, let us consider the notion of *marriage as a war.* This will increase your understanding of the stage on which the cast of characters in child-custody proceedings must perform.

The War

As a psychologist and marriage/family counselor, I am strongly committed to promoting healthy life styles. As you might expect, I must be aware of weaknesses in a marriage (such as the "craziness" of one or both of the spouses), but I always keep the view that there is the potential for positive relations. In other words, I am ready to perceive and to cultivate the strengths in even a stormy or weak marriage.

Given this professional set, it is somewhat difficult for me (and from their comments, I know this is true for many of my colleagues as well) to view marriage as a war.

To digress for a moment, I wish to emphasize that a psychotherapist or marriage/family counselor does not agree to "save a marriage"—except for certain counselors with religious affiliations whose religious beliefs hold that a marriage should continue, no matter how bad it may be. Rather, the approach is one of entering into the helping relationship for purposes of guiding the husband and wife to new understanding of how their marriage works, why there may be problems, alternative ways for them to feel and behave, and of teaching them techniques to change their behavior (such as learning how to communicate more effectively).

While many of us would like to believe that "marriages are made in heaven," it is self-evident that, in point of fact, marriages are made by society. In other words, marriage is a social institution, and like the structures for all social institutions, the structure of marriage can be changed. And change has occurred, as best exemplified by the ready option of divorce. More will be said on social changes in the structures of marriage and family later, when we discuss the changes society has accepted for child-custody determinations.

So with reluctance, I have to accept that marriage cannot be idyllic and that there will be battles. But what is the reason for this negative framework?

Perhaps one of the most basic facts is that males and

females are not the same. Quickly I should add that I consider myself to be staunchly in favor of sexual equality, but nevertheless there are differences—some biological and some very much a part of socially conditioned roles.

The differences between the sexes seem to bring an underlying dissonance to any heterosexual relationship, and because of the intensity within marriage, spouses obviously have to deal with them. In their book *The Longest War: Sex Differences in Perspective,* Carol Tavris and Carole Offir emphasize that males and females are not "like two sides of a coin" and that the two sexes "have regarded each other less as fellow human beings than as alien and exotic creatures—to be loved, feared, cherished, or confined." They go on to posit a warlike relationship:

> Men and women have wooed each other with lustful abandon and ritual restraint, but they have also fought—if not with military weapons then with psychological, economic, and sexual ones. The battle of the sexes began in the sleepy dawn of prehistory and has continued to the present. There have been countless alliances and dalliances across enemy lines, but the peace treaties never seem to last. It is truly the longest war. (Tavris and Offir, 1977, p. 2.)

And so sex differences, whether inherent to gender or societally imposed on the person as he or she grows up, have the potential of creating marital conflict.

Personally, I do not consider sexual differences to be the primary source for dissonance; I believe the individual characteristics of the husband and wife are more important. Each person has a unique personality structure. Foremost within the realm of personality, at least for purposes of creating and maintaining a marriage, is the *need system.*

We all have *primary* and *secondary* needs. Primary

needs involve the requirements to sustain life, such as food. Secondary needs are socially oriented and are learned. Perhaps the best way to clarify the nature of secondary needs is to present what Allen L. Edwards, a noted personality researcher, considers to be the fifteen most important needs:

1. ACHIEVEMENT: To do one's best, to be successful, to accomplish tasks requiring skill and effort, to be a recognized authority, to accomplish something of great significance, to do a difficult job well, to solve difficult problems and puzzles, to be able to do things better than others, to write a great novel or play.

2. DEFERENCE: To get suggestions from others, to find out what others think, to follow instructions and do what is expected, to praise others, to tell others that they have done a good job, to accept the leadership of others, to read about great men, to conform to custom and avoid the unconventional, to let others make decisions.

3. ORDER: To have written work neat and organized, to make plans before starting on a difficult task, to have things organized, to keep things neat and orderly, to make advance plans when taking a trip, to organize details of work, to keep letters and files according to some system, to have meals organized and a definite time for eating, to have things arranged so that they run smoothly without change.

4. EXHIBITION: To say witty and clever things, to tell amusing jokes and stories, to talk about personal adventures and experiences, to have others notice and comment upon one's appearance, to say things just to see what effect it will have on others, to talk about personal achievements, to be the center of attention, to use words that others do not know the meaning of, to ask questions others cannot answer.

5. AUTONOMY: To be able to come and go as desired, to say what one thinks about things, to be independent of oth-

ers in making decisions, to feel free to do what one wants, to do things that are unconventional to avoid situations where one is expected to conform, to do things without regard to what others may think, to criticize those in positions of authority, to avoid responsibilities and obligations.

6. AFFILIATION: To be loyal to friends, to participate in friendly groups, to do things for friends, to form new friendships, to make as many friends as possible, to share things with friends, to do things with friends rather than alone, to form strong attachments, to write letters to friends.

7. INTRACEPTION: To analyze one's motives and feelings, to observe others, to understand how others feel about problems, to put one's self in another's place, to judge people by why they do things rather than by what they do, to analyze the behavior of others, to analyze the motives of others, to predict how others will act.

8. SUCCORANCE: To have others provide help when in trouble, to seek encouragement from others, to have others be kindly, to have others be sympathetic and understanding about personal problems, to receive a great deal of affection from others, to have others do favors cheerfully, to be helped by others when depressed, to have others feel sorry when one is sick, to have a fuss made over one when hurt.

9. DOMINANCE: To argue for one's point of view, to be a leader in groups to which one belongs, to be regarded as a leader by others, to be elected or appointed chairman of committees, to make group decisions, to settle arguments and disputes between others, to persuade and influence others to do what one wants, to supervise and direct the actions of others, to tell others how to do their jobs.

10. ABASEMENT: To feel guilty when one does something wrong, to accept blame when things do not go right, to feel that personal pain and misery suffered does more good than harm, to feel the need for punishment for wrongdoing, to feel better when giving in and avoiding a

fight than when having one's own way, to feel the need for confession of errors, to feel depressed by inability to handle situations, to feel timid in the presence of superiors, to feel inferior to others in most respects.

11. NURTURANCE: To help friends when they are in trouble, to assist others less fortunate, to treat others with kindness and sympathy, to forgive others, to do small favors for others, to be generous with others, to sympathize with others who are hurt or sick, to show a great deal of affection toward others, to have others confide in one about personal problems.

12. CHANGE: To do new and different things, to travel, to meet new people, to experience novelty and change in daily routine, to experiment and try new things, to eat in new and different places, to try new and different jobs, to move about the country and live in different places, to participate in new fads and fashions.

13. ENDURANCE: To keep at a job until it is finished, to complete any job undertaken, to work hard at a task, to keep at a puzzle or problem until it is solved, to work at a single job before taking on others, to stay up late working in order to get a job done, to put in long hours of work without distraction, to stick at a problem even though it may seem as if no progress is being made, to avoid being interrupted while at work.

14. HETEROSEXUALITY: To go out with members of the opposite sex, to engage in social activities with the opposite sex, to be in love with someone of the opposite sex, to kiss those of the opposite sex, to be regarded as physically attractive by those of the opposite sex, to participate in discussions about sex, to read books and plays involving sex, to listen to or to tell jokes involving sex, to become sexually excited.

15. AGGRESSION: To attack contrary points of view, to tell others what one thinks about them, to criticize others publicly, to make fun of others, to tell others off when dis-

> agreeing with them, to get revenge for insults, to become angry, to blame others when things go wrong, to read newspaper accounts of violence. (Edwards, 1957, p. 11.)

The idea is that every person has these fifteen needs to some extent, but people vary as to how important a given need will be in their lives. For a stereotyped example, the top three (the highest) needs for a wife might be ORDER, INTRACEPTION, and AFFILIATION, whereas the top three (the highest) needs for the husband might be ACHIEVEMENT, AUTONOMY, and SUCCORANCE. When the couple marries, the obvious challenge is to blend their need systems into a complementary union.

To go a bit further on the importance of needs to marriage, the renowned personality theorist H. A. Murray points out that these needs create *press*. Stated simply, a wife's needs create a press on her to find fulfillment and a press on her husband to contribute to her fulfillment (because of the role he has contracted to play via entering into marriage). Needless to say, the husband's needs create the same kind of two-fold press in return.

What we have are two personalities coming together. Personality in marriage is clear-cut, even in a basic definition of the term. For example, the eminent psychiatrist Harry Stack Sullivan defined personality as "the relatively enduring pattern of recurrent interpersonal situations which characterize a human life." According to Sullivanian theory, such interactions are both intrapersonal (within the individual), as exemplified by fantasies and impressions of others, and interpersonal (between two or more people). Without doubt, marriage is the most intense "interpersonal situation" that most adults ever encounter, and consequently the making of a marriage is dependent upon the interaction of the husband's and wife's personality factors. This interaction is why marriage counseling focuses upon helping each individual recognize his or her own personal characteristics, such as what is needed from life in general and from a spouse in particular, as well as dealing with marital relations *per se.*

Given the intricacies and unknowns about personalities, the marriage of two persons introduces a highly complex situation. Thus, it is not surprising that there are often marital conflicts and that many times the conflicts cannot be resolved in a manner that will allow the marriage to continue.

It should also be acknowledged that many marriages continue, even though there is unhappiness and discontent. One research study estimated that less than 25 percent of marriages are fully satisfactory to both partners, and similar studies found that perhaps as few as 5 percent carried that kind of mutual satisfaction. Similarly, at any one point in time, less than half of existing marriages are rated as "reasonably adequate."

This dissatisfaction is known to create emotional and behavioral problems for both the adults and the children. I will deal with the specific problems brought about by divorce later (see Chapter 4). At this time, I will simply note that discontent creates the kind of press mentioned earlier, and this press requires psychological energy to combat. When psychological energy is exhausted or too much is demanded by the living conditions, emotional and behavioral problems erupt (several subsequent chapters will provide details on ego strength).

Divorce

Just as marriage was created by society, so too was divorce. At one time, divorces were difficult to obtain—difficult in several ways. First, legal requirements for a divorce were very strict and extremely adverse conditions had to be proved, and there were long waiting periods. Second, society frowned upon divorce. It was not long ago that a divorced person was spoken of in hushed tones in family circles, and there was clearly a social albatross around the neck of the divorcée.

Today the picture is different. Over the past two decades, there has been a long and rapid series of changes in divorce laws and, perhaps of greater importance, in societal views toward divorce.

Now one can obtain a divorce quickly and without evidence of gross wrongdoing on the part of either spouse. A person's divorce history cannot be required for employment or other situations that might result in discrimination against the divorced (a similar nondiscriminatory set is maintained, of course, for the married and never-married as well). And societal acceptance of divorce is such that most people do not have even a covert negative reaction when they learn a person is divorced, not to mention any overt rejection.

Divorce is now acceptable, even when it occurs more than once for a given person. It is so acceptable that many people believe there is a divorce epidemic.

Statistics from surveys by the United States Bureau of the Census, as well as data from many other sources, bear out that divorce is both prominent and increasing in today's American society. A few important facts from a 1976 survey are suggestive. The divorce rate doubled from 1964 to 1976. Most divorces, for both men and women, occur in the 45–54 age bracket. At the time of the survey (March 1976), there were 2.8 million men and 4.4 million women who were divorced and not remarried.

Obviously the increasing divorce rate has implications

for children. This is especially evident from the fact that divorces occur most often in the 45–54 age bracket. This is an age that would include persons past the child-bearing stage and who would, in all likelihood, be parents if they were ever to be parents.

It should be noted that there has been an increase in age of divorcing parents; this suggests that more and more children will be affected. Ten years ago, it was estimated that one out of six first marriages would end in divorce. Today the figure ranges in estimates of two or three of six first marriages. A decade ago, about half of divorces took place during the first ten years of marriage and about half of divorces were before there were any children. A 1970 study showed that 60 percent of all divorces included children. The increasing age for divorce has led to an increase in the number of divorces that involve children.

As will be elaborated upon later, having only one parent creates the possibility of some undesirable conditions for child development. It seems evident that more and more children are faced with the probability of being raised by only one parent. One family theorist asserts that one out of every six children lives in a single-parent home. In 1976, the aforementioned survey from the United States Bureau of the Census revealed that 3,718,000 children of divorce (under 18) were living with their mothers only and another 299,000 were living with their mothers as the head of a subfamily (i.e., some sort of reconstructed and/or amalgamated grouping). In addition, 340,000 children of divorce lived with their fathers alone and another 50,000 children were living with their father as the head of a subfamily.

These statistics show that four to five million children are unquestionably victims of divorce—victims in the sense that they have been deprived of the benefits of having two parents to raise them—and there are countless other children who have endured the adverse effects of a divorce and are in reconstructed families. Even reconstructed families, presumably with an adoptive replacement parent, leave the child to cope with the experiences and feelings associated with the real father's or mother's absence and with the changes associated with a new family system.

The Last Battle

The last battle of the marital war is child custody. Even when the custody decision is not contested, there is, in fact, a battle—but one parent simply surrenders early.

It is interesting that heretofore few custody decisions in the United States were contested. Ten years ago, it was found that only 2 percent of contested divorces were over children. While an exact figure for today is not available, there are all sorts of reasons to believe that the number of divorces contested over children is increasing and, moreover, that more child-custody contests are waged after divorces have been finalized. This latter is an important point and I will comment more extensively on it in the chapter on sexism in child custody (see Chapter 6).

This last battle—child custody—is the topic of this book. Throughout, I will attempt three things. First, I would like to help you understand all of the psychological and sociological implications of child custody. The implications will be for you as well as for your children. Second, I believe that we adults have erroneously harbored the notion that our best interests are more important than those of our children when child-custody determinations are to be made. This may be hard to admit, and it may have been kept at a subconscious or unconscious level of motivation, but I believe that it is true. I would hope that I can offer a new posture that will maximize the healthy aspects of child custody for both parents (including the one who does not get custody) and the children. Third, and finally, I recognize that many parents want to wage this last battle with as much armament as possible, and I will acquaint you with the criteria used by courts to evaluate parents for suitability for custody and will offer practical guidelines for mapping a custody-contest strategy (such as how to prepare for a custody fight and what kinds of allies you need) that will increase your chances of coming out a victor. While the old adage of "all's fair in love and war" does not apply, since professionalism precludes "dirty tricks," there will be a "no-holds-barred" approach to pulling ammunition from behavioral science.

2.
I'll Keep the Car, You Keep the Kids

THE WORD "CUSTODY" carries a connotation of possession. While most parents would argue that they seek custody of their children because of love, devotion, and a wish to safeguard and care for them, in point of fact, the motives are often not so altruistic.

Lawbooks do not provide a precise definition for "custody." Several analysts of court records have pointed out that custody is a slippery word and that the courts do not always use it to cover the same thing. As will be illustrated in several different ways in this book, the entire decision-making process for child custody is highly subjective. That is, few, if any, objective and/or quantifiable ways exist for determining with whom the child should be placed.

What actually happens is that custody is defined in a unique manner with each case. The basic construct—placing the child with an adult—stays the same, but the factors considered and evaluated for making that placement decision and the conditions for continuing that custody differ according to each particular situation.

Without belaboring a definition, "custody" can be considered to be a method for varying relations, rights, and duties. Relations are varied by prescribing visitation rights or with whom the child will reside. Rights are varied by specifying living conditions and financial-support plans. And duties are varied by the court's making it clear what the mother and the father must each provide in some manner for the rearing of the child, regardless of with whom the child is living.

Custody is also (and perhaps foremost) a governmental action. It is difficult to accept that a parent-child relationship can be determined by something as abstract as a governmental system, but this is the heart of child-custody determinations.

Legislation is created that mandates certain duties and rights for both parents and children. This legislation specifies authority to the legal system for upholding these duties and rights. Executive decisions about violations and fulfillment of these duties and rights are made by professionals deemed by society to be responsible (such as law-enforcement officers, social workers in public agencies for children, educators, and health professionals). Like marriage and divorce, child custody is a social institution created and maintained by the government.

For the purposes of this book, I will confine my discussion to custody between natural parents. As I will bring out in detail later, society has moved toward the position of questioning that custody by the natural parents is an inalienable right. The contemporary view is that what is in the best interests of the child may be more powerful than a parent's natural right to custody of his or her own child. While I will focus on aspects of a custody battle between natural parents (as a way of keeping the material organized), essentially all of the points made about what factors are evaluated for custody determinations and how a person can go about winning the battle for custody of children can be applied to foster parents. In addition to foster parents with no blood ties to the children, this material is applicable to relatives, like grandparents and aunts and uncles, who would like to get custody of children within their extended family.

So to wrap up this brief coverage of definitions, I would suggest settling on the following: *Child custody refers to the decision made either before or during legal divorce proceedings between the natural mother and natural father as to with whom the child should be placed,* with the alternatives usually being either the natural mother or natural father or another guardian, such as foster parents.

The Good Old Days

Looking back over the years, we find child-custody decisions were once quite different from what they are today. In order to better appreciate the current state of affairs, a look into the past seems in order.

Several centuries ago, philosophers routinely considered the family not just a personal but a political unit, even to the point that the details of rearing children were considered to be of fundamental concern to society as a whole. And family life patterns were viewed as important to the structuring of civil government.

Historically, the primary sociopolitical stance was that there was a "parental right to custody," meaning that any biological parent was entitled to custody of his or her children. The only exceptions were parents who were clearly shown to be unfit. For the most part, the courts rather naively followed a few simplistic notions of morality and natural affection.

Not only have "parental rights" given way to "children's rights," but there has been a noticeable movement toward greater governmental control of how family life patterns will be maintained. In other words, in the past family life patterns seemed to influence the structure of the government, whereas today the government seems to influence the structure of the family.

Probably the best example of this governmental control is that laws prescribe what parents are expected to do for and with their children. That is, to keep the parent-child relationship free from governmental intervention, parents must fulfill duties.

Parental duties include providing children with financial security, living conditions that are conducive to health (mental and physical), opportunity to receive an education, and relations that will bring about values of morality, social respect, and legal behavior. When I talk later about the rights of children, more parental duties will emerge.

One of the foremost considerations for child-custody determinations in the "good old days"—that is, in past centuries—was economics. Children were viewed by the courts as being of monetary value.

Custodial rights had commercial value, particularly in the feudal period. The concept of children as chattel was so well entrenched that custodial rights could literally be transferred and sold. As might be assumed, children were important as workers in early agricultural societies and for fulfilling servantlike roles.

A good illustration of how courts considered the chattel rights to be more important than other factors is found in England in the early 1800s. An eight-month-old girl was spirited away in the night from her English mother by her French father "almost naked in an open carriage and in inclement weather." The mother wanted the father prevented from taking the child away from her and out of the country. The court held that it would protect the child from detriment, but since this child had not "been injured for want of nurture, or in any respect," the father was entitled by law to the custody of the child. In other words, the father's claim of property/chattel rights (because of "male supremacy") was held to be more powerful than a mother's relationship to her child.

I should quickly add that this economic factor did not have unquestioned endorsement. It was often subjugated, even two centuries ago, to protecting the welfare of the child. For example, at the same time that the aforementioned English case occurred, another English case resulted in the father being refused custody because of "alleged immoral conduct and way of life and unpopular political and religious views." Of course, we don't really know if this decision was to protect the welfare of the child or whether it was to punish the father by removing property of value, i.e., his child, because he behaved and thought in a manner unacceptable to the political and moral attitudes predominant in England at the time.

In earlier days, therefore, the legal principle was that the father had the paramount right to the custody and control of his children. The husband and wife were considered to be one source, and that one source was the husband. Blackstone, the great legalist, said that "a mother as such is entitled to no power but only to reverence and respect." While a father was viewed as having natural right to child custody, the mother's right was recognized only upon the death of the father.

Things Aren't the Same as They Used to Be

The notion of "parental power" has been replaced by "parental duty." My earlier comments on governmental control mentioned the basic framework for parental duties. That is, parents have the fundamental duty of supporting, protecting, educating, and rearing their children in a manner considered to be moral, right, and legal by our contemporary society.

This shift from parental power to parental duty has monumental legal and social implications. The foremost implication is the basic rationale for making custody determinations. The power-to-duty shift has resulted in the "best interests of the parents" being replaced by the "best interests of the child" as the primary legal basis for deciding with whom the child will be placed. The next chapter will deal exclusively with the concept of the best interests of the child.

Just as there has been a shift in whose interests are most important, which has resulted in changes in priorities among factors that are evaluated and considered in child-custody determinations, so too have there been alterations in the governmental system that establishes and maintains child custody.

Today, family relationships are not prescribed by heritage or religion but by legal concepts. American society, predicated on individual freedom, has not jealously guarded individual freedom for parent-child relations. Numerous social analysts have asserted that, from a legal perspective, the parent-child relationship is probably the least secure in the family constellation. For example, the government cannot take any legal steps to terminate or even readjust an ongoing husband-and-wife relationship unless at least one of the spouses agrees to it. On the other hand, the government has a variety of steps possible for terminating or readjusting parent-child relationships.

This is not to say that governmental regulation of the parent-child relationship is bad. Indeed, given the complexity of American life and all of the problems commonly encountered, it may well be that our society requires this much (or maybe even more) governmental regulation of family life. I tend to think that this is the case. But in accord with our commitment to democratic processes, we must always be alert to the possibility of regulations that were benevolent in intent resulting in invasions of privacy or the deprivation of individual constitutional rights.

In a nutshell, a parent can expect to remain relatively free from governmental intervention by fulfilling the obligations or duties. These are in a constant state of flux and are defined by abstract values that evolve in our society. As our society evolves through different stages of science, technology, and cultural sophistication, new standards for living emerge and are put forth as community expectations for behavior. Laws are the general avenue for establishing these expectations and standards, and the human services endorsed by society—medicine, law, education, psychology, social work, etc.—implement actions that can lead to regulations and controls. When these standards are applied, any event in the life of either the child or the parent is subject to question. At this point in time, the societal standards are unrelentingly enforcing the rights of children and the duties of parents.

3.
Power to the Children

FUNDAMENTAL to the shift from parental power to parental duty is the recognition that children are persons. Under law, children have minimal rights, at least compared to adults. Consequently, the fact that divorce and child-custody statutes are beginning to recognize the interests of children is highly significant from a legal-philosophical point of view.

The idea that minors should have no legal rights is rooted in the same kind of archaic reasoning that maintained that women should have fewer or different rights from men or that certain races should have less legal status than other races.

In the last chapter, I mentioned that society sets forth expectations and standards for parenting, and that governmental control, through laws, creates a system by which parents are literally judged for how well they fulfill their societally determined roles. Stated simply, *society declares that children have rights within a family.*

There is no definitive set of rights for children. Moreover, there is no single legislative authority that has, to date, established the rights of children, as distinct from the rights of all American persons.

We are left with a situation that requires us to deduce from logic, philosophy, and relevant laws exactly what a child has the right to experience. As I move shortly into discussing the concept of the best interests of the child, certain legal ideas will be presented to clarify how parents are expected to function in relation to their children. It is these expectations that end up being part of the legal decision-making for custody determination, and it is important that they be translated into fairly exact criteria (a task which will receive extensive coverage in Chapters 7 and 8).

At this point, I believe it is sufficient to look at a so-called "Bill of Rights for Children" created by two law professors, Henry Foster and Doris Jonas Freed. They believe that, based on social morality and law, a child has the following rights:

> To receive parental love and affection, discipline, and guidance, and to grow to maturity in a home environment which enables him to develop into a mature and responsible adult;
>
> To be supported, maintained, and educated to the best of parental ability, in return for which he has the moral duty to honor his father and mother;
>
> To be regarded as a person, within the family, at school, and before the law;
>
> To receive fair treatment from all in authority;
>
> To be heard and listened to;
>
> To earn and keep his own earnings;

> To seek and obtain medical care and treatment and counseling;
>
> To emancipation from the parent-child relationship when that relationship has broken down and the child has left home due to abuse, neglect, serious family conflict, or other sufficient cause, and his best interests would be served by termination of parental authority;
>
> To be free of legal disabilities or incapacities save where such are convincingly shown to be necessary and protective of the actual best interests of the child; and
>
> To receive special care, consideration, and protection in the administration of law or justice so that these best interests always are a paramount factor. (Foster and Freed, 1972, p. 347.)

I should emphasize that these are merely opinions from two law professors, but they do seem to reflect the intent of child-custody statutes, as will be evident soon.

The concept of the best interests of the child has already been mentioned several times. At one time, child-custody determinations were based on the "best interests of the parents" (originally, in America, the interests of the father, and later the interests of the mother). This concept later evolved to the "best interests of all the persons involved," whereby children started to be considered. In turn, today's guiding framework is that of the "best interests of the child," whereby the welfare or interests of the child are held to be the most important consideration or even the only one.

The concept of the best interests of the child provides the court with a framework for making custody decisions. The concept results in three assumptions. First, certain behavior can be detrimental to a child's welfare to the point that a parent should lose custody for letting that behavior occur. Second, consideration should be given to the wishes of both the parents and the children. And third, the noncustodial parent has virtually no duties except providing financial support. These assumptions get translated into what is called the fitness test. That is, each parent is evaluated by the court (presumably using evidence from medical, behavioral science, and educational professionals) to determine which parent is better able to meet the best interests of the child.

The concept of the best interests of the child underlies a rather revolutionary societal position toward natural parents. In their controversial book *Beyond the Best Interests of the Child,* Joseph Goldstein, Anna Freud, and Sidney J. Solnit (1973) argue—quite persuasively, it seems to me—that natural parents have no special claim on custody of their children. Natural parents are referred to as "biological" parents, and are considered to be potentially less appropriate for custody than "psychological" parents (i.e., adults with a sincere, affective, loving, positive relationship with the child). Of course, natural parents can also be psychological parents, but psychological parents need not always be biological parents. Their primary point is that they consider that the best interests of the child can extend beyond an allegiance to the biological parents, and they believe that the best interests of any child can probably best be maintained by psychological parents, regardless of presence or absence of blood relationship.

This preference for the psychological parent over someone who is simply the biological parent has been incorporated into state child-custody statutes. Further, it is being progressively implemented in cases which heretofore would have guaranteed custody to one of the natural parents. For example, the Nebraska Supreme Court recently affirmed a lower court's decision that removed a two-year-old boy from the natural parents and declared that the right to parental custody and control is a natural but not an inalienable right. The boy was placed in a public home for children because the court thought he would receive better treatment there than he could receive from his natural parents. When I describe the criteria applied to custody decisions (Chapters 7 and 8), you will see other evidence of how the concept of the best interests of the child has led to priority being given to the psychological parents rather than to the biological or natural parents.

The inclusion of the concept of the best interests of the child into state statutes gained impetus from the Commissioners on Uniform State Laws' 1969 Uniform Child Custody Jurisdiction Act. This prestigious legal group offered legal guidelines for safeguarding the child in a custody dispute by considering mental and physical well-being ahead of parental interests. On the basis of these guidelines, individual states have started amending existing or creating new state statutes that will express the concept of the best interests of the child.

There are numerous exemplary state statutes. For instance, Michigan has enacted a statute that is a fine example of how criteria for deciding child-custody questions should be evaluated, should be in the best interests of the child, and should encompass information from a variety of professionals (such as psychologists, social workers, and educators).

The Michigan Child Custody Act of 1970 declares that the most fundamental concern should be the best interests of the child and that there are specific criteria that provide a "sum total" of evidence that will be "considered, evaluated, and determined by the court."

The Michigan Act has excellent specificity, as evidenced by the following criteria that must be evaluated:

- Love and affection between parent and child;
- Emotional ties between parent and child;
- Capacity of parent to give child guidance;
- Capacity of parent to continue educating and raising the child in its religion or creed, if any;
- Capacity of parent to provide food;
- Capacity of parent to provide clothing;
- Capacity of parent to provide medical care;
- Capacity of parent to provide remedial care;
- Capacity of parent to provide other material needs;
- Length of time lived in an emotionally or psychologically stable, satisfactory environment and the desirability of maintaining continuity;
- Permanence of proposed custodial home (geographical stability);
- Moral fitness of parent;
- Mental health of parent;
- Physical health of parent;
- Home record of child;
- School record of child;
- Community record of child; and
- Child's preference for parent (if court deems child sufficient in age).

These criteria reflect that the best interests of the child cannot be ensured by the simple assumption that the natural parents automatically provide the best care for the child. In fact, the child's best interests may not be able to be met by the natural parents.

The Michigan Child Custody Act sets the stage for several points I will present later. First, the criteria include information that must come from sources outside of the legal system. Most notably, information is needed from behavioral scientists (such as psychologists, social workers, and sociologists), educators (such as teachers and counselors), and health personnel (such as psychiatrists, other physicians, and nurses). Second, you should be getting an idea of the factors you will be dealing with when you map a strategy for winning the custody battle. In other words, if you are anticipating an involvement in a custody battle because of your own marital war, then these are the types of factors to which you will need to tailor both your offensive and defensive tactics.

In Chapter 1, I mentioned that children have traditionally not had an attorney, much less any special advocates from behavioral science, education, or health services, in child-custody legal proceedings. Only the parents have had legal counsel and have been free to bring expert testimony to help their individual efforts to get custody of their children.

Legal counsel for children is a major breakthrough in child-custody laws, and one that you, as a parent, must both accept—even if it seems counter to your personal preferences and interests—and demand on behalf of your children. Moreover, we are into an era where many lawyers, because of professional ethics, will feel obligated to adhere to the concept of the best interests of the child, even if you (as their paying client) would like them to give primary emphasis to your interests.

Throughout the last decade, there have been many court decisions that have held that children are constitutionally entitled to the guarantee of due process, and this means right to legal counsel. While most of these decisions have been in juvenile courts where a child or youth is being tried for criminal offenses, the legal principle also supports the right to legal counsel in child-custody legal proceedings.

The concept of the best interests of the child seems to make it imperative that the child be offered the opportunity to have legal counsel. Because of the potential threat of this type of action to both parents and because of the expense, it seems likely that some parents will resist this move. Of course, the essence of "positive parenting" is helping the child. Parents who tried to deny their child legal counsel might be viewed by the court as possibly unfit on those grounds alone.

Until such time as the courts rule definitely that a child must have his or her own legal counsel—as opposed to the parents' lawyers supposedly protecting the best interests of the child in their representation of their respective parent-clients—it seems likely that few children will enjoy their right to legal counsel. Of course, the failure of divorcing parents to provide their children with legal counsel may invite more governmental intervention; perhaps governments will begin providing legal counsel to children as a public service.

4.

Old War Wounds (And a Few New Ones, Too)

DIVORCE creates problems for everyone in the family! If you have seriously contemplated divorce or if you have gone through a divorce, that statement may seem too obvious to be necessary. But it is well documented that few people who enter into a divorce realize the emotions that they will experience and the problems that they will encounter because of the divorce.

However, it is beyond the scope of this book to discuss why people divorce and how they can best cope with the many problems that arise from the divorce. We must concentrate on the single issue of child custody.

To gird oneself for the battle for the children, three things need to be understood.

First, it is necessary to recognize how the social, psychological, and physical development of the child is dependent upon relationships with parents, and to be aware of the psychosocial implications of divorce for the child.

Second, any stressful situation—and divorce would certainly fit that description—taxes anyone's ego strength, and divorce may create emotional and behavioral problems for both the adults and the children.

And third, it is wise to accept the reality that divorce does not end the relationship between the child and each of the parents. All divorce really does is end a social institution—the legal definition of marriage. The relationship will continue for the entire lives of all family members. It is a little difficult to accept, but even if the child should never see one of the parents after the divorce, the psychological aspects of the relationship continue on not only throughout the child's development but even into his or her adult life.

Growing Kids

Most adults, when looking back on their own childhoods, tend to marvel at how they survived (while at the same time often having idealized notions about how simple and easygoing their childhood period was compared to the complexity of today). Childhood is difficult, partly because the human organism is moving through developmental stages to the point where intelligence, neurology (and other physical factors), and personality are adequate to deal with life's demands, and partly because the child is a little person in a world of giants.

Needless to say, the child is dependent upon parents for sustaining life, acquiring learning, and experiencing happiness. No child's life will be (nor should it be) totally free from demands, stresses, conflicts, and so on, but it is up to the parent to protect the child from conditions with which the child cannot cope.

This brings us to divorce. Divorce is a solution for the parents, but it has an unquestioned impact on the lives of the children—perhaps even more than on the lives of the parents, since the children usually have less understanding of the reason for the divorce and are less able to work through the inner conflicts that are inevitably associated with the demise of the marriage and reordering of relations with the two parents.

Since divorce is an adult action that affects the children as well, responsible parents entering into divorce must understand what the children will be experiencing and how they can help the children through the turmoil and uncertainty of the divorce and readjustment. As a first step toward this objective, I would like to review some of the basic principles of child development. These are principles that apply to all children, whether or not they experience a divorce in their family. From this, I will move to what research says about problems that specifically stem from divorce.

Self-esteem or self-worth is probably one of the most basic personality characteristics. Regardless of how successful our lives may be in any sphere of living (be it education, work, or marriage), we must have an adequate degree of self-esteem or else we cannot optimally use our capabilities and attributes.

Research in both psychology and sociology is consistent in finding that divorce tends to reduce children's self-esteem. Moreover, it has been found that the younger the child, the greater the loss of self-esteem.

While there is no clear-cut age when the child becomes resilient to the impact of divorce on self-esteem, child-development theorists seem to accept that children are most vulnerable during the first eight years of life. I will discuss the susceptibilities peculiar to several childhood stages and relate these to the quality and consistency of nurturance.

The child from infancy to about two years of age must develop a sense of basic trust in the world and his or her self. This quality is fostered as the child's needs (e.g., food and comfort) are met with attentive and consistent caring, such as from parents. After acquiring a sense of basic trust, the child from two to four years of age will begin to gain a sense of autonomy—that is, a sense of his or her own separateness as an individual. Up until this time, the child hardly differentiates felt needs from those who fulfill them. During this period, there is considerable vacillation between asserting autonomy as an individual and reverting back to the symbiotic relationship with those who provide nurturance. At this time, parents assist the developmental process by accepting both extremes of behavior and yet by providing necessary and reasonable limits and encouragement for the toddler's growing sense of independence. Acquiring both basic trust and autonomy during these early years is critical to the child's later personality and self-esteem. The question is whether parents can maintain consistent nurturance that will meet such developmental needs, and I think we must acknowledge that divorce may bring about changes in parenting patterns and capacities.

When the child reaches age three or four, the psychological and physical aspects of the child are at a stage with unique susceptibilities. There is a tendency to fear the world. There is an expectation of abandonment and loss of the parent(s). Even if the child is not deprived of one or both parents, there is an incipient expectation that he or she will be rejected by the parent. In other words, there is a profound need for security, and failure to receive large doses of security-giving contacts with parents leads to problems that could potentially continue throughout the child's life. This is, indeed, a highly critical period for all children, namely because of the need for security and the vulnerability of self-esteem.

At age five or six, the child has begun to move through this susceptibility to insecurity and has started to identify directly with the parents. This has both positive and negative implications. On the positive side, the child accepts the parents into his or her self, thereby gaining much-needed strength to counteract anxiety that is inherent at this stage of development. On the negative side, there is a marked increase in awareness of differences between the two parents, and the child is torn between the two parents; the child doesn't know with which parent to identify. The mother, probably because our society has typically cast her into the primary parenting role for this age, has a special attraction to both boys and girls, while at the same time there is an infatuation with the father. Children now have a very special pull toward the parent of the opposite sex. At the same time, they sense that there is a union between the mother and the father, and they feel that if they move as close to the parent of the opposite sex as they would like, the parent of the same sex as the child will resent it; they feel that they will lose that parent's love, that they will be punished, and that they must be wrong for having these feelings about the parent of the opposite sex. In other words, the child of five, six, or seven experiences mass contradictions of feelings and a proneness toward being self-deprecating and having guilt.

It is easy to recognize how a divorce could affect a child in either of the two stages. A divorce could have a severe handicapping effect, one that could last many years and could affect the child's relations with others, be it friends throughout childhood and adolescence or persons considered to be potential marital choices in adulthood. In my work as a psychotherapist, I have encountered numerous persons with marital problems, such as distrusting their spouses or feeling incapable of being adequate adult-spouses themselves, and as they unraveled their histories, it became clear that many of these feelings were rooted in their feelings toward and experiences with their parents in the four-to-six-year age period.

As the child moves to the next stage, perhaps at age eight or nine, there seems to be a bit of relief from the psychological pressures of growing up. This seems to last until the child is ready to enter puberty and adolescence. While a whole array of new pressures arises at this time, perhaps around age twelve or so, the child has, of course, learned a lot about coping with life, and research supports that—all other things being equal—divorce can be more readily handled by adolescents than by younger children.

Regardless of age, nurturance is an important source of ego support. It is so important that I have speculated about the possibility of this being a requirement for the continuation of any marriage. From my clinical practice, I know of no case where divorce occurred in the presence of much nurturance, but I can think of countless cases of marital dissonance (some resulting in divorce) where one or both spouses complained about a lack of nurturance from the other.

Nurturance involves caring. The caring is, of course, more than merely providing material things, be it new cars or food. It is the communicating of respect, warmth, and love for the welfare of the person being nurtured. All of us have some degree of nurturance—this is an important need. Because of the evolution of each of our need systems, however, people vary in how much nurturance they need to give and to receive. The marriage relationship, as I suggested in the discussion in Chapter 1, is predicated upon mutual need fulfillment. Consequently, the husband and wife need to be able to give and receive nurturance to an extent that is compatible with each of their needs. The fulfillment does not have to be exact, nor to a specific dosage, because there can be compromises or adaptations between needs. That is, if one need is fulfilled in a rich fashion, it seems likely that another need could be fulfilled to a lesser degree than would be optimal. For example—and at the risk of sounding as if I exaggerate the importance of the sexual need—I have often found that couples whose sexual needs are richly fulfilled can usually accept less than preferred fulfillment of other needs.

Children have a strong need for nurturance. While this is probably most profound through early childhood—say, up to age eight—it continues into adolescence. As might be expected, parents are the primary givers of nurturance to children, whereas the adolescent progressively moves toward people outside the family (such as friends) for nurturance until finally selecting a spouse for the role of primary nurturer. This supports the oft-heard notion that people marry someone to replace their mother or father. They certainly do, at least in the sense of accepting someone for the need-fulfillment role that was once played by the mother and/or father.

Nurturance is seriously jeopardized by divorce. To date, in our society, the mother has been relegated to the role of primary nurturance-giver, and divorce decisions involving children tend to support the view that separation from the mother probably has greater potential for psychological trauma for the child than would separation from the father. Courts have historically favored placement of the child with the mother, often even in situations where the mother probably could not provide the child with as desirable conditions as the father or a foster home. More will be said about preference for the mother over the father in Chapter 6, and more will be said about factors that lead courts to make custody decisions in Chapters 7 and 8. At this point, suffice it to say that the loss of or decrease in nurturance for the child carries a high risk of psychological stress. Unless this is effectively counteracted, problems will ensue.

Identification is another significant factor in the early-childhood development stage. As mentioned, the child has mixed feelings about both parents. Regardless of the sex of the child, there is vacillation back and forth between the mother and the father for identification purposes. At one point the child imitates and wants to be just like the father, and rather abruptly there will be a shift toward imitating and wanting to be like the mother. All of this vacillation or shifting is both normal and desirable. It is through this testing and trying out of the father's and mother's characteristics that the child can learn what characteristics and behaviors hold strengths and weaknesses for his or her own uses. This is an important step in developing capabilities for coping with life.

Identification is affected by divorce. For example, if a child is placed with only one parent, regardless of whether it is the father or the mother, there is no opportunity to experience intimately the identification processes prompted by the other parent's characteristics. The belief that the child needs two parents supposedly motivates many a parent to remarry. While that might not be the best reason for selecting a new spouse or for entering into another marriage, it does indicate that parents are aware that children need to identify with two parents. Obviously children can and do survive without two parents, but the benefits of learning (as well as the possibilities for need fulfillment) are fewer with only one parent.

Faulty identification development, such as might occur with the child who has experienced intimate contacts with only one parent (and with no other parent substitutes), can influence behavior in later life. As but one example, it is well established by research that one's outlook on work, including vocational choice, and attitude toward persons of the opposite sex, as enters into dating and marriage, are heavily influenced by the identification processes with parents during early childhood.

Parental absence has received considerable attention in research on child development. Divorce and child-custody placements create parental absence, and research reveals that parental absence has a strong impact on the child's general development and especially on the child's personality. Obviously the child's personality determines innumerable things later in life, not the least of which is his or her ability to get along with and derive satisfaction from other people, be it on the job or in a marriage.

Does it matter which parent is absent? That is a question that research has not yet answered properly.

As will be brought out in Chapter 6, our American society has chosen to award the custody of children almost exclusively to the mother. Though this is rapidly changing, research studies have consequently focused on the effects of the father being absent; there is little information on the effects of the mother being absent.

As a most basic guideline, research from developmental psychology suggests that the absence of the same-sex parent is particularly important—that is, that it is critical to boys if the father is absent and critical to girls if the mother is absent. The basis for this finding is the identification model just discussed.

One might assume that because of this important identification model, child-custody determinations should award the boys to the father and the girls to the mother. This is too simple a rule. As we will see later in discussing the criteria used in custody determinations, this identification model has entered into court decisions, but oddly enough, usually only after the child has reached adolescence—a period far beyond the critical stage of development when identification with both parents is most important.

The age of the child at the time of the parental absence has also been the subject of research. In brief, the mother's presence or absence seems most critical in infancy and early childhood. As I suggested earlier, however, this may be simply because mothers have been relegated to the role of primary care-givers by our society. In this era in which many fathers are assuming new care-giving roles within the family, research may reveal that the sex of the parent who is the primary care-giver with infants and young children is irrelevant. Middle childhood—ages eight to twelve—seems to be when the child is most vulnerable to the father's absence. Again, however, the stereotyping of parental roles for both mothers and fathers in our society, to date, really makes much of the research almost meaningless. At best, it would seem that these findings might afford some insight into processes critical to certain ages, such as nurturance and identification, but they scarcely merit being viewed as facts.

Regarding both issues—the sex of the absent parent and the age of the child at the time of parental absence—I am left with the belief that research has not clarified the matter and that, in all probability, it does not matter whether it is the mother or the father who is absent; the absence of either parent can have negative effects, and the age of the child means little because there are particular vulnerabilities at every age that can be affected by either parent's being absent.

Battle Fatigue

Divorce messes with the minds of all persons involved—the parents and the children, and to a lesser extent, presumably, grandparents, aunts and uncles, and other relatives. Why does it mess with the mind? Because it attacks personal security, saps ego or psychic strength, creates uncertainty, and fosters self-doubts.

Divorce is affect-laden, to say the least. This is not to suggest that divorce is bad, because obviously many marriages create conditions for adults and children alike that can have far worse effects than a divorce. But it is meant to suggest that when divorce occurs, it is only honest to recognize that it will not be easy. Emotional and behavioral problems will likely erupt, some for only brief or transitory periods, others perhaps for a very long time.

While the parent may feel overwhelmed with coping with his or her own problems, it must always be remembered that the child is under the same pressure and that it is up to the parent to step in and assist the child in coping with the stress. This is a requirement of responsible parenting.

Nathan Ackerman, one of the foremost family theorists, clearly suggests the relevance of mental problems and divorce:

> The frequency of divorce of childless parents is of no great consequence to the evolution of society and family. Di-

> vorce involving the fate of offspring is the more vital question. In the latter instance, marital conflict is of significance not only of itself but also as the epitome and the very core of disintegrative trends in family life and the harbinger of distorted emotional development in the offspring. Ultimately this distortion adds to the burden of mental illness in the community. (Ackerman, 1958, p. 149.)

As painful as it may be, this statement captures the essence of the following discussion. That is, it is not divorce *per se* that we as a society have to be concerned about. Rather, it is the fact that the divorce symbolizes that there have been conditions, such as unresolvable marital conflicts, that have had disruptive effects for parents and children and that the family life has disintegrated. This, in itself, could be viewed as an emotional or behavioral disease, with divorce simply being the term for the overall unhealthy condition. But, as I will try to bring out in Chapters 5, 9, and 11, there are ways that the risk of emotional and behavioral problems can be lessened.

In approaching the problems that can potentially come out of divorce, I am purposefully avoiding an esoteric analysis of the psychodynamics that a child experiences. That would contradict the objective of a pragmatic understanding of the problems associated with divorce and relevant to child custody. I would, however, suggest that anyone interested in a comprehensive in-depth look at the special crises and everyday problems that divorce causes children might want to read *Children of Divorce* by J. Louise Despert and *The Parents Book About Divorce* by Richard A. Gardner.

Psychiatric problems in both parents and children seem disproportionately higher for those involved in divorce situations than for those with no divorce in their lives. There is, however, a subtle issue here that needs to be clarified before discussing specific problems. That is, there seems reason to question whether it is the divorce that causes the problems or whether it is really a matter of personal limitations within the parents that allow the problems to come out with both them and their children during the divorce. Perhaps another way of saying it is that it would seem feasible, if not probable, that mature, mentally healthy parents could divorce—such as for reasons of personality incompatibility or value differences—and still maintain an allegiance to their children in such a manner as to avoid undue emotional or behavioral problems for all concerned. Unfortunately, such is not usually the case.

In infants and very young children, much research on maternal deprivation has revealed that there is a strong emotional dependency that must be fulfilled. It is fulfilled by touching and cuddling, words of love and affection, and, of course, caring for physical needs. Children who have been deprived of this type of loving care (which could presumably be given by either a father or a mother) have suffered a variety of emotional problems, and these, in turn, have led to countless behavioral or adjustment problems. This research can be applied to divorce.

If divorce results in the child losing "tender loving care," or even having a significant lessening of such care, there is a high risk of the child's experiencing an anxiety reaction, which might be both psychological and physiological. This could take the form of sleeplessness, temper tantrums, irritability, poor eating habits, and a host of physical complaints and illnesses and many forms of personal insecurity. In fact, emotionally deprived infants have been known to literally wither up and die, even with their physical needs being met, from a disease known as marasmus.

Depression and a lack of interest in the world around them are also frequently found with children of divorced parents. It is easy to see how the disintegration of the psychological world—their family—could lead to gross feelings of insecurity and a distrust of others. The child reasons, "Why get involved with anyone? If my own mother and father can fall away from me, so can anyone else."

Research has shown that children with divorced parents have a higher incidence of poor school performance and delinquency than children whose parents are both with them.

While I have singled out several problems that seem to be the most commonly encountered among children of divorced parents, these are certainly not all that could occur. One psychiatric study found that children of divorced parents suffered essentially all of the same kind of emotional and behavioral problems found with disturbed children, and they have a higher incidence of problems than the average child or a child from a home with both parents.

What is the cause? Aside from having parents who may themselves be less able to cope with conflicts and problems than parents who remain together, the child is placed in a situation that has tremendous implications for self-esteem. In most divorce situations, it is virtually impossible, except when there are healthy, supportive parents, for a child to weather the divorce storm without decreased self-esteem.

Since the legal system does not provide for the child's mental-health needs during the divorce period, the high risk of the child's developing emotional and behavioral problems underscores the need for both parents to accept the responsibility of aiding the child, even though they themselves are carrying a heavy emotional load.

I have made several references to parents also suffering and encountering problems during the divorce. Since our focus is children, it seems inappropriate to elaborate on this point. More will be said, however, about adults coping with divorce in Chapters 5, 9, and 11.

Research indicates that approximately three-fourths of divorced women and two-thirds of divorced men have emotional and behavioral problems to the point that they must seek professional help from a psychiatrist, psychologist, or social worker. Most commonly, their problems center around depression, anxiety, mood swings, irrational reasoning, and conflicts with others (such as breaking laws or fighting with people at work or with friends and family).

There is, of course, great similarity between the problems suffered by divorced parents and their children. As you might expect, the causes are essentially the same—namely, both parents and children are under such great pressure and experience so many conflicting thoughts and feelings that massive insecurity sets in. In the next chapter, I will offer a few ideas about how this high risk can be lessened and how parents can take steps to safeguard both their own mental health and their children's.

5.
The Cease-Fire Line

THE MOMENT the divorce decree is final, many (probably most) parents declare, "Thank God that's over!" Little do they realize that the relationship with the ex-spouse is far from over. The relationship will continue to affect the lives of both ex-spouses (as well as any new spouses that may enter the situation in the future) and the children to some degree throughout their lives. They have only reached the "cease-fire line."

In reality, divorce typically ends only two aspects of marital life. The first is the day-to-day contact that marriage involves. The second is the sexual intimacy that is primordial in marriage.

Even in these two areas, however, there are exceptions. One research study found that approximately 31 percent of divorced parents continued "repeated and intensive interaction . . . during the two-year period following the divorce decree" As a psychotherapist, I have heard of numerous situations in which the divorced couple continued to have contacts, often sexual in nature. While they might explain that the contacts are "for the children," it seems more likely that they reflect a need for continuing the relationship in some fashion.

Granted, these observable contacts and their effects typically decrease with time, simply because each divorced parent is establishing his or her own individualized way of living. In so doing, they often are moving away from each other both figuratively and literally. They are developing new interests and values different from the ones they shared. And, of course, they generally start making new friends, including someone who will replace the former spouse as a primary need-fulfiller.

Regardless, the effects continue, and it is important to accept the long-range implications of the relationship with the divorced spouses—even if explained as being "for the children."

Divorce, then, is a process, not an event. The divorce does alter the family relationships on a day-to-day basis. As one child recently explained it, "Now I have to do something with one of them, either Mom or Dad—I wish we could do things together again." That comment touches on a critical factor. The child's keeping contact with separated parents, which is desirable and essential (if possible to arrange), keeps the child's thoughts in a "family framework." The child harbors, often on into adulthood, the fantasy that someday his or her child-world, with the security afforded by the previously unified family, will be recreated. In some cases this fantasy becomes a source of neurosis that will have to be unraveled with a psychotherapist in either childhood or adulthood, or it may provide motivation for the person to formulate his or her own adult life (such as concepts of the ideal spouse and family life) so as to resolve the conflicts and insecurities created by the parents' divorce.

Divorce is, when reduced to basics, merely an adjustment of relationships. Divorce does not erase the past, and, therefore, the experiences of the past will influence the future. As a clear example, research shows that second marriages are made stronger through learning from the mistakes of first marriages. Similarly, divorce does not rule out influence from the past marriage on future attitudes and behaviors. To take a strong example, if a divorced husband disappears and provides no financial support to the children, despite a court decision, the attitudes of both the mother and the father may be affected. The mother may begin distrusting and not depending upon others, and the father may begin to feel he does not have to fulfill responsibilities and can disobey legal specifications.

With the children, divorce definitely does not end any relationship. There will merely be altered relationships with each parent when custody is awarded. The child may now have only the mother taking care of and disciplining him or her on a day-to-day basis, and may see the father only for visits to parks or feasts of ice cream on Sunday afternoons. The possibility for distortion of identification processes and the development of unhealthy views toward relationships with others is readily evident in this admittedly stereotyped, but very common, custody picture.

Earlier, I mentioned that each parent's influence would continue, even if one of the parents was totally removed from the lives of the ex-spouse and the children. The past, both the good and the bad, will live on in the minds of all, and will influence the present and the future. Of course, this is true in other parent-related situations too, such as when a parent dies.

Keeping Your Head on Straight

It's hard to be honest about divorce and child custody without facing up to the fact that some undesirable results can come out of the affair. As I have said, this does not mean that divorce is bad. Indeed, it may be an improvement (especially in the long run) over a destructive marriage and family life. But it does mean that smooth sailing will not come automatically. As you contemplate divorce and child custody, it is necessary to chart a purposeful course, and this means being prepared for the possibility of rough waters. Given the material in the last chapter on the risk of emotional and behavioral problems for both parents and children, the next task is to plot and steer your course to your advantage.

If all I have said about the psychological aspects of child development seems obvious to you or if you think you thoroughly understand the child-development ideas I presented, then you are one giant step toward being prepared to help your children through the divorce and child-custody crises. As will be apparent in the later discussion of the criteria for making child-custody decisions, those professionals who play key roles in evaluating parents for capability of meeting the best interests of the child—lawyers, psychiatrists, psychologists, and social workers—believe that one of the most important criteria for the custody determination is the parent's ability to provide child guidance. This underscores the importance of being academically prepared to assist the child's efforts to handle the negative aspects of the divorce. Reading psychology materials (and there are some excellent self-help books today) is important. Regardless of experience and training, we all need to continue striving for better understanding of human behavior, particularly that of ourselves and those to whom we are responsible, such as our children.

As well as an understanding of child development, it is necessary to have some skills so that you can actually step in and help your child. Knowledge and action are not the same. A lot of people know what to do, but still cannot do it. If you are a parent involved in divorce, then you will be making a substantial commitment of your psychic energy or ego strength to keeping your own emotional house in order. It is to be hoped that you will have energy to spare for your child and will not be blind to your child's need for your support. If you are seeking custody, you must establish your capability of meeting the needs of your child, and exercising your responsibility via helping your child cope with the effects of the divorce will speak well for you.

Another prerequisite to handling the disruption of the divorce is to be prepared for the battle. More will be said on this matter in the discussion of actual strategies and tactics for fighting for custody of the children, but I will point out now that a major ingredient in battle-readiness (as any military strategist will attest) is one's state of mind or outlook.

The appropriate outlook is one that is at all times grounded in reality. People often naively think, "If I keep it out of my mind, it will be best," or "If I don't tell anyone about it, I can handle it myself." There may be instances in which the above reasoning is appropriate, but in a divorce, it would be very unwise.

You should accept that the divorce and the ensuing

months will not be easy. Obviously, it might be a relief to have your ex-spouse out of the way and to have the legal negotiations settled, but there will be countless thoughts and situations that keep the past bad marriage alive. It is wise, then, to accept that all of the bad cannot be erased immediately. Sorting through your experiences for ideas about how to avoid similar problem situations in the future and for understanding of your thinking and behavior can be a rewarding process.

It is desirable to get all of your questions and feelings—anger, insecurities, guilt—out in the open for yourself. While this may mean sharing them with another person, such as a relative or friend, you have to be careful not to allow this verbal ventilation to turn into a neurotic confessional. In other words, some people babble on and on about their past marital problems and their present personal crises, not to attain resolution, but to get sympathy. In the process, they end up being reinforced for their weaknesses, rather than gaining new strengths. Do not let yourself wallow in self-pity or rely excessively on the sympathy of some seemingly well-intentioned friend or relative. The task is to accept, analyze, and eliminate the problems, and above all, to preserve ego strength and cultivate new resources in the process.

After taking steps toward insight, you should carefully map out routes to self and social rewards. I have seen many persons avoid divorce (at some pretty high prices of suffering in a bad marriage) or crumple psychologically during the divorce (thereby hurting themselves and their children) primarily because of the lack of sources for ego strength. For all its shortcomings, a marriage does usually give a sense of identity and, consequently, ego strength; this allows the person to muddle through. When the divorce comes, all of the sources for ego strength associated with the spouse are eliminated, often rather abruptly. Replacements that improve upon the old sources must be found quickly and wisely.

Self and social rewards come from doing or experiencing things that are pleasurable (or at least are not unpleasant). These may constitute seeking self-satisfaction alone, such as by pursuing hobbies or avocational interests or turning inward for spiritual strength (many persons in divorce find religion to be helpful). More likely, it may mean getting involved with others in ways that will bring responses from them that will make you feel worthwhile and needed.

The idea of "staying busy" is all too often dismissed lightly. Several years ago I was involved in a research project in two large hospitals where the research team studied patients who were depressed. We had them become involved in crafts, hobbies, and recreational activities with an occupational therapist and also provided them with psychotherapy directed at their depression. Somewhat to our surprise, a fairly sophisticated psychological method for measuring the effects of the two treatments (occupation therapy versus psychotherapy) revealed that the depression was counteracted more by simply being active than by participation in psychotherapy. This finding has been borne out in other studies as well. This does not mean that psychotherapy has no benefits for the depressed person. It does, and for some depressed people, psychotherapy may be the preferred treatment. What the research means is that activity is better than inactivity, particularly when the activity involves social contacts with others. This point has special importance to persons in divorce, since depression is one of the most commonly experienced emotional reactions during and after the divorce.

All social activities are not the same. Throughout my years as a psychotherapist, I have been struck by how frequently divorced people are frustrated in their attempts to have social contacts, with the outcome often being increased suffering and anxiety.

In planning social activities, it is essential to remember the objective: mental health. That alone will eliminate a number of activities. One divorced man told me that he just could not seem to make friends, even though he tried every night. It turned out that he did try every night, but what he did was go to a bar and drink to the point of becoming obnoxiously drunk; even other drunks avoided his company.

Plunging into dating behavior creates another potential pitfall for the divorced person. In meetings of organizations for single parents, I have sometimes observed something almost like mass hysteria. I have seen males and females alike act and talk in ways that I know (from other contacts with them) were totally dishonest and unhealthy. I have watched them pair off when it was evident that the pairing had no logic, had the potential of being unhealthy or not in either person's best interest, and was simply a frantic attempt to establish some kind of contact with another person, even a highly superficial, potentially destructive relationship. These same kinds of episodes occur in a variety of settings, including church groups, dance clubs, and the like.

Sexual activity, because of the intimacy and strong feelings it entails and the associations it usually carries forth from the disintegrated marriage, has the potential to exert powerful positive and negative influences. There may be two quite opposite reactions. Either the divorced person goes through a phase which may be brief or may extend over many years of wanting nothing to do with sex (including masturbation), or he or she may enter into sexual activity in a frantic or reckless manner.

Eliminating sexual activity from one's life is appropriate, probably for everyone, at some times. On the other hand, abstinence can be inappropriate and maladaptive. For most people, biological, psychological, and social factors combine to create a true need for sexual release. In our society this is typically with a person of the opposite sex.

Given a bad marriage and the fact that the sexual relationship is almost always a focal point in the disintegration (but not necessarily the cause of the problems), many divorced persons harbor unhealthy feelings about sexuality and may project them inappropriately onto others. You should avoid generalizing the negative sexual relationship with your ex-spouse to all other persons of the opposite sex. New partners will not enter into sexual activities with you in the same way, unless, of course, you consciously or unconsciously arrange your relationship with them in such a way that they can only become involved with you sexually in the way you disdain.

If you leave a divorce with distrust for members of the opposite sex or a wish "just to be left alone for a while," it would be understandable—but only for a period of time. If your past life has been heterosexual and if sexual activity has the potential for bringing you rewards—and I believe the latter is true for essentially all persons—then there will be a point in the not too distant future when you should allow your sexuality to emerge and be fulfilled again. This might start with masturbation, with the idea that fantasies of a lover can cultivate positive attitudes for persons of the opposite sex, and eventually progress to actual intimate relations with another person.

Some divorced persons pursue an unreal notion that sexual activity will solve all of their problems. Again through my psychotherapy contacts, I have met many divorced persons, both males and females, who leave the divorce court and virtually jump into bed with the first person they see. In several adult dance and social clubs for single parents, the routine pattern seems to be to bounce into the room, try to look charming and sensuous (even if this is not the real you), drink too much alcohol too fast, sort through a couple of prospects, leave with someone (even if it is not a very desirable pairing), stop for a cup of coffee and a sandwich, go to one apartment or the other, have sex, leave, wake up the next morning feeling futile and depressed, and then see your therapist in the afternoon to lament about how the world is doing you wrong.

It must be understood that any pairing that is to be constructive, with or without sexual activity, must be meeting a healthy need. It is very easy to enter into self-defeating behavior that fulfills a neurotically conceived need.

To clarify, one divorced man told me of his whirlwind courtships, which occurred several times each week in the sequence described above. He sought treatment because he would end up in the bedroom with some female he had met an hour or two before, they would undress, kiss, fondle—and he could not get an erection! This failure to perform was especially painful for him because his entire life style was predicated on the macho image—tough, aggressive, virile. As we analyzed his life, it became evident that he had been told sex was dirty by his mother, that girls who seemed to enjoy sex in an uninhibited fashion frightened him, and that his ex-wife had forcefully laid out expectations for him, be they in work, child care, or sex. He simply could not handle females who spoke with authority, respected themselves, and enjoyed sex. His sexual inadequacy was related to his overall personality, and it, in turn, had been badly battered by a stormy marriage that had recently ended in divorce. His first order of business was not to find sex partners—since he had had about twenty undressed and wanting sex in a three-month period, it was clear that this was not his problem. Rather, his goal was to prepare himself to enter heterosexual relationships in a comfortable healthy manner.

The foregoing comments on pursuit of sexual activity should not be construed to mean that I believe sexual activity should not begin right after the divorce. Depending upon their values and need systems, some persons can and should enter into "sex for sex's sake," meaning there might be a minimal, if any, affective relationship with their sexual partners. In these cases, though, the healthy person does not distort reality, does not see sex as the cure for all problems, and accurately perceives the sex partner as not promising anything beyond the immediate sexual release. Most persons continue to feel the challenge to build an all-encompassing better life regardless of momentarily satisfying sexual episodes. I had one female patient (who held a master's degree in psychology, so should have known better!) who would make a casual pickup in a bar, have sex with the person, then call a real-estate agent the next morning to go look at houses for them to "live in when we're married," although she knew full well that she would probably never see the male again. This is a true neurotic delusion. Fortunately, she gained insight into how she could start meeting males in places that would increase the chances that she might have compatibility with them, such as at universities and professional conferences, and she soon met and married a professional man—but she didn't look for a house until they were engaged.

A final self-created step is to adopt a positive view toward the future. Acquiring the "power of positive thinking" is more easily said than done, but without it, things will be very difficult. You must accept that you have had problems, that life could have (perhaps even should have) been better. But it was not better. And it is now time to make things better. Achieving this goal requires two qualities. First, you must truly believe that you can make things better. And, second, you must be prepared to work seriously toward improving your lot in life. This will take self-sacrifice in the sense of giving up the temptation to pursue some crazy notion which might promise quick relief (such as self-defeating behavior like alcohol consumption, sexual promiscuity, or suicide). Rather, you must stay steadfastly committed to building a better life style gradually. I will say more on this in Chapter 11.

Thus far, most of my suggestions have emphasized self-help. There are times when professional help will be needed. Since the problems associated with divorce and custody crises are commonly emotional conflicts and behavioral disorders, this means turning to a psychiatrist, psychologist, social worker, or marriage counselor for help.

Not all psychiatrists, psychologists, and social workers have specialized training in the areas of concern to you, namely marriage and family problems. Having a doctor's degree does not guarantee ability to deal effectively with the intricacies of marriage, family, divorce, and custody problems.

A few states have licensing laws; in such states the telephone-book yellow pages will list "certified" or "licensed" marriage counselors under the heading "Marriage and Family Counselors." Since this category is infamous for including self-ordained marriage counselors as well, it is probably best to seek a professional who has two credentials. First, he or she should be licensed or certified as a psychiatrist, psychologist, or social worker. Second, and of most relevance to our purposes, he or she should be a "Clinical Member" of the American Association of Marriage and Family Counselors. This association, a nonprofit professional organization, conducts a nationwide accreditation program for practitioners of marriage and family counseling. To be a "Clinical Member," the professional, regardless of how many academic degrees he or she has, must have documented specialized training in and successful supervised practice of marriage and family counseling. More information, including the names of "Clinical Members" in your locale, may be obtained from the American Association of Marriage and Family Counselors, 225 Yale Avenue, Claremont, Calif. 91711.

Finally, marriage and family counselors differ in the theories and techniques they use. Reputable marriage and family counselors will tell you readily about their preferred approach and how applicable it is to your needs. If you wish to read about different techniques, you might wish to look through *Sexual, Marital, and Familial Relations,* a book on professional-practice approaches which I wrote with my wife, Dr. Jane Divita Woody.

6.
The Gladiators: The Mamas and the Papas

OVER THE YEARS in the United States, custody of children has customarily been awarded to the mother, often when all evidence indicated that the father had the greater potential for caring for the child. There has been an unwritten assumption, particularly in the last century, that a child of "tender years" (to use a nebulous legal phrase) should be placed with the mother.

Estimates vary, but it appears that over the last few decades, mothers have received custody in approximately 80 percent of the cases. Fathers have received custody in about 10 percent of the cases. In the remaining 10 percent, children have been placed in a variety of situations, such as with both parents, with relatives, or with guardians appointed by the court.

Since our society has deemed that females should earn less money than males for the same jobs and should be ineligible for certain kinds of employment, it has proved logical for the mothers to receive custody. In fact, fathers have been quick to accept this position, often because they wanted their children to have the best conditions that money could afford and knew that being free from the duties of childrearing would allow them to work and earn more money for the support of their children. In his book *Psychiatry and Law,* Ralph Slovenko describes the situation well:

> The father as a rule recognizes that the mother can render better care, the children usually wish to be with the mother, and consequently he does not request child custody or possession of the family home in the divorce action. The mother is literally the house-keeper. It is observable among the human and animal species that it is generally the mother who cares for and protects the young. The father may also recognize that a custody dispute is to be a futile endeavor. Surveys of sample cases indicate that maternal custody is awarded in 85 to 95 percent of the cases. (Slovenko, 1973, p. 361.)

Incidentally, there is still academic dispute as to whether the female of the species, be it human or animal, has biological determinants for child care or whether the customary female role results from social conditioning. The male of the species is usually the stronger, which contributes to meeting physical needs (such as catching animals to eat or earning money in a wider variety of jobs than the female). Because of physical limitations, the female of the species has usually cared for the home-nest and, consequently, the offspring. As society sees fit to free both males and females from stereotyped roles, such as who will be the breadwinner and who will be the housekeeper, there are indications that commitments to and capabilities for childrearing will undergo marked changes.

Because of this tradition in the child-custody courts,

many parents move through divorce with the assumption that the child-custody decision is predetermined—that the children will be placed with the mother. But going back several centuries, as I mentioned before, the father was held to have a nearly absolute right to custody in a "property rights" sense of the word. His right to custody was removed only where danger to the child or corruption of the father was proved.

As a present-day rule of thumb, mothers are normally preferred for child custody for children of "tender years." The court rulings do not define "tender years" specifically by age, but presumably it could be any minor age. It seems that the older the child becomes, the more tendency there is to place the child with the parent of the same sex.

Heretofore, major exceptions to placing the child with the mother have been when the mother has proved to be "unfit," usually because the father has been able to establish himself as far superior in potential for rearing the child (wealthy professional men, such as lawyers and physicians, have been the most successful at combating the preference for placement with the mother) or because the mother engaged in some sexual indiscretion. One is left to speculate whether the decisions against mothers who have had sexual activity outside the marriage are to protect the children or whether it is society's way of punishing those who violate its sexual mores.

The introduction of state child-custody statutes predicated on the concept of the best interests of the child paves the way for major shifts in custody determinations. In other words, these statutes make it clear that the gender of the parent and the biological link between the natural parents and the children are not as important as the best interests of the child.

Recent trends in sexual-equality laws also point toward revisions in the criteria that will be applied to child-custody decisions. These laws posit that males and females have equal constitutional rights to work and live, and they certainly seem to extend to the child-custody arena. Thus mothers and fathers have a constitutional right to equal consideration for possible child custody.

Despite the rather clear-cut laws, I must admit that most states have yet to practice what their laws preach. One of my recent clients was a father seeking custody of his five-year-old daughter. Educationally, he and his wife were similar. He held a doctorate in a social science and was a professor at a state college. His wife held a master's degree and was a public school administrator. Both had seemingly healthy overall histories, except for unquestionable marital incompatibility and for her alleged involvement in extramarital sexual activities. Further analysis of their work schedules revealed that the father spent a considerable amount of time at home preparing his lectures and was regularly available when his daughter needed him (such as if she were sick during the day). The mother, on the other hand, was gone a great deal of the time. Her job required many night meetings in the community, and she also seemed to enjoy socializing away from the home more than he did (on weekdays and weekends alike). She was assuming that she had a right to custody, and he was contesting on grounds that he could provide the child with better care and a stronger, more dependable parent-child relationship. This was in a state with a child-custody statute that was patently aligned with the concept of the best interests of the child. When the father's lawyer got the case before a judge, the judge responded, in effect, "I don't care what the state law says today, we all know that a little girl's interests are best served by being with her mother, and as long as I am judge, children of this age will be placed with their mothers."

While this is but one true case, a lawyer friend of mine did a research survey among the circuit judges in that state and found that they were, in fact, avoiding the implementation of the law. As various professionals analyze the situation, it appears that this stance is based only on the personal biases of the judges and it does, in fact, contradict the law.

The foregoing story illustrates how important the characteristics of the persons involved in the custody battle are to the outcome. As I will report in later chapters, my research reveals that judges, lawyers, and the many professionals who can provide expert information or testimony in a child-custody case may well evaluate the situation according to their personal beliefs, rather than according to objective evidence. Parenthetically, since child-custody cases cannot be appealed to the federal courts, they are particularly influenced by the values and mores of the geographical area, and so the court in which the case is to be tried must be carefully selected. That is, you should try to get the case heard in a jurisdiction that reflects the values and attitudes toward parenting that will prove to be to your and your child's advantage.

The preceding comments might paint a rather bleak picture for the father who is seeking custody of his children. To date, the comments are accurate. On the other hand, there are many indications that in the future the picture will be different. Indeed, courts are already implementing the concept of the best interests of the child in ways that make it obvious that mothers no longer have a preordained decision in their favor. From here on, it will be a matter of establishing that you can best meet the interests and needs of the child, and the following material is directed at preparing you for this quest, whether you be a mother or a father.

As will emerge when I discuss offensive and defensive strategies for the child-custody battle, you need to have allies. The best allies will be high-status professionals—such as lawyers, psychiatrists, psychologists, social workers, and educators—who can present evidence on your behalf to substantiate to the court that you are better prepared than your ex-spouse to help your child through being awarded custody. I will be going into the subtleties of the "experts" and the criteria they evaluate in later chapters. At this time, however, your understanding of professional views toward the mothers (the champions) versus the fathers (the challengers) can be enhanced by reviewing some research I conducted with six hundred lawyers, psychiatrists, psychologists, and social workers. I will only summarize the research findings in this chapter. If you are interested in the research design and statistical details, you might want to read my article "Sexism in Child Custody Decisions," which is listed, like other works I have mentioned, in the back of this book.

First, I inquired, "If all conditions are equal, should a mother be preferred over the father for placement of a child?" While almost half of the professionals said she should be, it was not powerful support. I interpreted the data as suggesting that professionals still harbor the notion that mothers are better prepared to care for children, which may well be true because of societal factors, but that professionals were nevertheless becoming more open to alternatives.

For the preceding question, I analyzed the responses according to the characteristics of the professionals, such as their age, years of experience, professional discipline, and so on. The discipline of the males was not related to their opinions. For the females, I found that female psychiatrists, by far, expressed the strongest support for placement with the mother, and below them, the order was female psychologists, female social workers, and female lawyers. In practical terms, this means that, as a general rule, if you are a mother wanting a female advocate, one who will probably take a firm stand in your favor and be less open-minded to your ex-husband's wish for custody, you should hire a female psychiatrist to provide expert testimony. On the other hand, if you are a father and want a female advocate (and it might be a good tactic to have a female advocating a male for custody), you would be more apt to find support among female lawyers and possibly among female social workers and female psychologists, but you should probably carefully screen female psychiatrists for being open-minded to your getting custody.

Bear in mind, however, that other factors help determine how effective an expert can be on your behalf. For example, there are status differences among the disciplines. Right or wrong, of the four disciplines cited, psychiatrists enjoy the highest status, followed by psychologists. But faulty communication or even appearance can negate the status factor of the discipline. One law professor told me of a judge who postponed a hearing because he did not like the "mod" clothing worn by one of the lawyers; the judge had commented, "This case will be heard when all of the lawyers are wearing clothes, not costumes!"

In addition to the professional discipline seeming to affect the views expressed in favor of the mothers, I found that the professionals' ages and their marriage histories were related to how they viewed the mother versus the father. While there are no doubt exceptions, it would appear that the older the professional person is, the more apt he or she is to favor the mother. In addition, married professionals tended to favor the mother. Also I found that never-married professionals revealed the most opposition to placing the child with the mother.

The practical implications are clear. If you are a mother seeking custody, you should locate an older, married female (preferably a psychiatrist). If you are a father seeking custody, you should probably seek a younger, never-married female social worker to be your professional advocate. Keep in mind that the data did not reveal differences for the men according to professional discipline. I would be inclined to believe that the age and marriage-history factors are probably the same for both men and women professionals.

Another question in the research study was: "If all other conditions are equal, should the child be placed with the parent of the same sex?" Most of the professionals thought that same-sex placements did not matter. Analysis of their answers revealed that their views were not related to whether they were male or female, but were related to discipline. Psychiatrists gave the greatest opposition to placement with the parent of the same sex. Professionals, regardless of discipline, who had never been married and/or who were not parents gave greatest endorsement to placement with the parent of the same sex.

Practically speaking, if you wanted to base a custody claim on your being the same sex as the child and wanted a professional to speak on your behalf, it would seem—whether you are a mother or a father—that you would want someone who had never been married and/or who was not a parent. On the other hand, if you are trying to combat the idea of same-sex placement, you might want to consider having a psychiatrist provide testimony on your behalf.

My personal view is that expert testimony would probably have less importance in this kind of situation than the age of the child. As I have mentioned, the older a child is, the more likely it is that the decision will place the child with the parent of the same sex. Again, there can, of course, be many other factors that influence this decision, and in the overall picture, this is probably only a secondary factor (the most important factors will be discussed in the next chapter).

I inquired about preference for natural parents over a foster home, also of limited importance. As might be predicted, the professionals were heavily in favor of placement with the natural parents, if all else were equal.

Of great importance, I gleaned a list of twenty factors from the lawbooks that had been used through the years to make decisions about child custody, asked the professionals to rank-order them, and inspected their answers to see if personal characteristics influenced their opinions. I will discuss the preferred "top twenty" factors in Chapter 8, but it is important to note that there were personal characteristics that led the professionals to consider certain factors to be more important for one parent than for the other. In other words, there seemed to be a certain sexist quality to preferences for factors. Stated simply, sexism would be preference toward a parent in child-custody proceedings because of the parent's sex, not because of the issues directly relevant to the custody case.

Professionals from each of the four disciplines—law, psychiatry, psychology, and social work—revealed differences in preferences for the mother versus the father. Numerous factors were involved and specific biases according to discipline will be noted in Chapter 10, since you must be aware of possible biases when you recruit your allies for the custody battle.

The research findings on this matter are not clear enough to allow me to offer distinct guidelines. However, the data do reveal that professionals, even though they may possess prestigious credentials and many years of experience, are not immune to personal bias.

A major source of personal bias in the expert testimony of professionals seems to be rooted in their views of and attitudes toward the roles considered right for a mother versus those considered right for a father. Like all people, highly trained professionals tend to evaluate clients or parents according to what society thinks is "good behavior." The professional evaluations for child-custody determinations are no exception.

To safeguard yourself and your children, you should be aware (and make sure your legal counsel is aware) of the fact that even professionals can be biased in their views.

Before professionals are selected to give testimony on your behalf, they should be examined by you and your attorney as to how they think and feel about the criteria for decision-making that are presented in this book. If they cannot specify their views or will not discuss the matter, then forget them and seek another professional.

Remember that the custody determination is a critical situation, one that will affect you and your child's entire life, and this is no time to stand in awe of professional credentials. Investigate the professionals!

Moreover, the professional, whatever his or her discipline, should be able to apply evaluation methods that are objective—that is, evaluation methods that are relatively free from bias.

While you might be tempted to want to bias the outcome in your favor, keep in mind that it is in your best interest to produce honest evidence of your capability for meeting the best interests of your child. If you are not truly the better parent for this responsibility, your own integrity and the welfare of your child demand that you acknowledge your limitations and set about to work out a custody decision that will both meet the needs of your child and allow you to progressively develop a healthy involvement with the child, even if the child is placed with your ex-spouse.

I will be saying more about selecting professionals to provide expert information and testimony at other points in this book. For now, the main message is to watch out for personal bias, even among experts!

Despite this strong warning, I want to leave the subject on a positive note. I am convinced that our society is geared up to eliminate sexism from child-custody proceedings. While this may mean that fewer mothers will receive automatic custody and that eventually more fathers will receive custody, mothers and fathers alike should be pleased that the democratic process is finally assuring justice under law in child custody. In the long run, there is no doubt that this will prove to be to the advantage of mother, father, and children. Some professionals may still hang onto stereotypes about mothers and fathers and these may result in less-than-objective evaluations, but professionals are prepared to make crucial evaluations of the parent's potential for meeting the best interests of the child. The challenge to you as a parent is to strive to have any child-custody legal proceedings in which you are involved conducted in an honest, fair, academically astute manner.

7.
The Battle Plan

THE PRECEDING CHAPTERS have, I hope, made you aware of the many psychological and sociological aspects of divorce and child custody and introduced some of the factors with which you must deal when you move into the courts.

The American legal system is complex and often difficult to understand and accept. For such an important system, perhaps the system with the utmost power in our lives, the court and its laws can be surprisingly vague and ill-defined.

This arbitrariness seems especially personified in judges, and since judges (not juries) make child-custody determinations, any parent entering into child-custody legal proceedings should be prepared to recognize the judge for what he or she represents. Note that the judge should not be viewed as a "person," even though the judgment rendered is often highly personalized (such as reflecting the judge's values about parenting, as in preferring the mother over the father in the face of contrary evidence). The judge should be viewed as a "role," a seat of justice. Any attempt to conceptualize a judge differently will lead to negative effects. You must respect the judge and accept the authority society has vested in that position.

This chapter sets the stage for "choosing your weapons." And Chapter 8 will review the foremost factors that go into the evaluations for deciding which parent should receive custody. In a sense, these "top twenty" factors will be your weapons for waging the custody battle. At this time, however, I believe it is essential that you survey the battlefield—the court.

Here Comes the Judge

My comments above emphasize that the judge must be respected and that the judgments must be honored. Judicial decisions are the law, and any attempt to avoid, deny, or subvert them must be viewed as pathological and would, in most cases, be subject to penalty. Therefore, for your own welfare and the welfare of your child, you should enter the battlefield steeled to accept the outcome and, even should it prove to be less than desired, prepared to work and live constructively after the dust settles.

Aside from the authority of the judge, perhaps the most major consideration for the proceedings will be the jurisdiction of the court—in other words, where the battle is staged.

As mentioned earlier, domestic law cases, such as child-custody legal proceedings would be labeled, are not generally subject to federal law, except in cases appealed on the basis of constitutional rights. So anytime you hear some angry parent who has lost custody cry, "I'll take it to the United States Supreme Court and get my child back," forget it. This is the futile expression of the frustrated, angry parent trying to cope with the emotional pressure.

Child-custody cases are heard in state circuit courts and may potentially be appealed to the state supreme court, but only if there is adequate legal justification for an appeal. In almost every instance, regardless of state, the decision will be made by a single person—a judge. Juries are not used in child-custody cases.

As stated, custody cases cannot ordinarily be appealed to the federal courts unless some constitutional right is being pleaded. For example, it is feasible that a custody hearing in the state circuit courts could be alleged to violate federal constitutional protections, such as denial of due process or the right to counsel, etc. In such an instance, a writ of *certiorari* would be filed, which means the federal courts would decide whether the writ presented questions that were sufficiently worth considering. Granting the writ says nothing about the merits of the case *per se.* Thus, while it is theoretically possible to appeal to the federal courts, such an option would be difficult to attain and scarcely merits your contemplation.

Any judge or court has a prescribed jurisdiction. Stated simply, in child-custody cases the term "jurisdiction" refers to two things—what the law states about conditions for the child (such as what is required to earn custody) and what geographical area will be served.

Geographical area is a source of frequent misunderstanding. It is not uncommon to hear a parent seeking custody say, in effect, "Maybe the judge here denied me custody, but I'll move out of state and get custody, dammit!" Again, this statement is erroneous and simply expresses frustration.

Law professors have told me that "jurisdiction" is one of the most nebulous and complex legal terms in the American legal system. In fact, *Black's Law Dictionary* declares that jurisdiction "is a term of large and comprehensive import, and embraces every kind of judicial action." Again the breadth of the concept is emphasized, and this only serves to increase the potential for misunderstanding. However, a couple of points will provide adequate insight into its implications for child custody and help us avoid unnecessary confusion.

First, the courts do not welcome any attempt to bypass one jurisdiction in favor of another for purposes of trying to gain a desired decision. They consider this to be creating jeopardy for the children and insulting to the courts. So if a parent did move from one state to another, the probable result would be a rebuff and information back to the original court that would not help that parent at any point in the future when the custody conditions were reviewed.

Second, there has been a nationwide effort to standardize child-custody laws. In the Uniform Child Custody Jurisdiction Act created by the Commissioners on Uniform State Laws in 1969, the primary purpose of the act is stated to be to "avoid jurisdictional competition and conflict with courts of other states in matters of child custody which have in the past resulted in the shifting of children from state to state with harmful effects on their well-being." The act also promotes cooperation between states and works to "assure that litigation concerning the custody of a child takes place ordinarily in the state with which the child and his family have the closest connection and where significant evidence concerning his care, protection, training, and personal relationships is more readily available."

While it is true that each state and, indeed, each court is reasonably free to declare its jurisdiction, the preceding position statement has greatly influenced and reflects the general attitudes of most courts. Of course, should a court declare a jurisdiction or lack thereof that seems wrong, an appeal can be made.

According to a major legal source, the most basic guideline for child custody is "that jurisdiction exists if the child and the parents are domiciled in the forum state." If such reasonably permanent residence is not the same for each parent and the child, then the whole issue is open to debate and can be taken to the court to decide.

In choosing the battlefield, you obviously want to be in a court that has an inherent value system that will be compatible with the weapons you choose. In other words, the child-custody decisions rendered by judges reflect, to a significant degree, the social values and mores of the immediate locale, and you would logically want to appear before a judge who would be favorably disposed or at least open-minded to the factors on which you want to base your case for why you deserve custody.

I hope I have made it clear that you cannot play games with the jurisdictional matter and that your efforts should be in the best interests of your child. You are free, however, to do two things.

First, if there is any uncertainty as to where the jurisdiction is placed—that is, where the case must be heard—then you should consider alternatives. You should investigate the general posture of each possible jurisdiction toward the factors on which you will base your case. Consulting with an attorney in each area is one good method, but a preferred first step would be to have your primary attorney advise you on options and characteristics of specific judges and their past decisions.

Second, if the jurisdiction is clear-cut, but if you think that there is evidence that you cannot receive a fair hearing in that locale, you are free to petition for a change of venue. Again your attorney should advise you on the appropriateness of this action and the probability of your request's being granted. Since people readily understand the term "venue," they erroneously assume that it can be easily accomplished. However, there has to be a valid reason to change the jurisdiction. Usually it happens only when a judge is self-disqualified.

Where the Judge Is Coming From

Many judges, with all due respect for their scholarship and wisdom, make decisions that are subjective and that may, on occasion, reflect their personal values as much as or more than the law and facts. On the other hand, the large majority of judicial reasoning is based on the specifics of the law and the facts of the case at hand. Both the law and the facts, however, are considered in the context of so-called "precedent cases."

Precedent cases create "common law." Common law does not come from legislation *per se.* Rather, common law reflects the actions that were taken by courts or judges. From these previous cases, principles and rules of law are derived and applied to new cases. While it is feasible that precedent cases could reflect the idiosyncrasies of one judge, which could establish a principle or rule of law that would be unjustly perpetuated in later decisions, this is not usually the circumstance.

Common law provides the interpretive guidelines that

reflect the regional or local social values and mores, but such guidelines are typically consonant with the legislation underlying the given state's child-custody act. If such decisions are not in accord with the state law, other jurisdictions soon put them asunder and/or they are appealed and declared invalid.

As a way of understanding the judge's (and the opposing lawyer's) frame of reference for implementing the state child-custody act and evaluating the best interests of the child, I would like to review ten primary dimensions:

- Preference for the natural parents;
- The successful party in divorce;
- The relative weight of the claims of the father and mother;
- The morals of the parents;
- Other factors relating to the parents' desire and ability to care for the child;
- The child's wishes;
- The race, religion, and social views of the parents;
- The effect of a contract by the parents governing custody;
- The putative parent; and
- Available alternatives in the framing of the decree.

Be aware that these dimensions cut across the "top twenty" factors or "weapons" I will talk about in the next chapter.

Preference for the Natural Parents

I have made other comments about the natural parents versus the psychological parents. Of particular importance is the fact that contemporary interpretation of the concept of the best interests of the child, as discussed in detail in Chapter 3, is more and more viewing natural parenthood as no special condition. This view accepts that natural parents may not be able to meet the best interests of the child as well as other persons might be able to, such as those who can establish and maintain healthy psychological relations with the child, and that the natural parents, therefore, have no special claim on the custody of children.

This has not always been so. Historically, the "right to possession" has been applied and one of the natural parents was almost always preferred over others for placement—unless there was strong evidence that both natural parents would jeopardize the welfare of the child (and many times the definition of jeopardy was changed to allow for leeway or benefit of the doubt for natural parents).

"Desirable treatment" is a term often encountered in court decisions about the right of natural parents. In other words, can one of the natural parents provide the desired conditions for meeting the best interests of the child?

What is deemed desirable is based not on the parent's value system, but on the values of society. While a natural parent is most often chosen for custody, there are cases where it seemed as though one or both of the natural parents could provide reasonable care consistent with their own style and standard of living, but the courts decided that it was unacceptable according to the standards of society. A natural parent who had a "bohemian" life style lost custody to grandparents who had a "conservative" life style. A natural father lost custody because the court thought it best for the child to be "identified with the maternal side of the family" and so placement was with the deceased mother's brother. In addition, the courts have held that continuity of placement is more important than returning the child to a natural parent who became able to care for the child after an initial placement had been made. Of course, these cases are exceptions, but they do reflect what courts may consider in a custody case.

The Successful Party in Divorce

Given the usual hurt and disruption that occurs, it is difficult to think that there might be any "successful party" in a divorce. "Successful party" means the one to whom the divorce was granted. In the past, the notion of the successful party was important because it established that the "fault" for the marriage failure was on the shoulders of only one of the spouses. More recently, however, society has entered the era of "no-fault" divorce; divorces can be granted without either spouse being held responsible for the failure. Since the no-fault approach is rapidly becoming predominant, it seems likely that the notion of the successful party will soon fade away.

Through the years, child-custody determinations were occasionally based on the successful-party decision. In other words, if fault was fixed on one of the spouses, the other had a stronger chance of getting custody of the children. However, since the mother has usually been almost an automatic recipient of custody, the successful-party issue has not arisen often. When it has come up, it has frequently been used against the mother, especially in cases where the mother was proved to be adulterous (but proved adultery has not always kept the mother from getting custody).

The Relative Weight of the Claims of the Father and Mother

The relative weight of the claims of the father and mother is an issue closely aligned with the extensive discussion in Chapter 6 about possible sexism in child-custody determinations. Sexism in this context refers to preference being given to a parent in a child-custody case because of the parent's sex, not because of the issues directly relevant to custody and to meeting the best interests of the child.

In the past, the father did have a nearly absolute right to custody, but this was later replaced (in the last hundred years particularly) with an almost equal degree of absoluteness for the mother's right to custody. The mother's right was especially strong with children of "tender years." Since I have already discussed this matter extensively, suffice it to say that you should remember how important this historical posture was and still remains in the minds of judges. The concept of the best interests of the child clearly opposes giving primary significance to the sex of the parent.

Relevant to this factor, my research on attitudes of lawyers, psychiatrists, psychologists, and social workers indicates that overall these professionals do not differentiate between the mother and the father in terms of the criteria deemed to be important for evaluating suitability for child custody. As I cautioned before, however, there are exceptions to this finding, both within the ranks of judges and in the four aforementioned disciplines, and so you should be alert to any possible bias against equal treatment for mothers and fathers.

The Morals of the Parents

Morals are often the basis for decisions in common law. Morality seems to have entered primarily in cases where mothers were sexually promiscuous and/or had an affair outside of marriage.

Adultery, when proved, has often resulted in the mother's losing custody, even if she was seemingly "fit" in every other manner and if there would be no reason to think that her adultery would, in fact, jeopardize the children. In view of the harshness with which morals and adultery have been used against mothers in child-custody cases, I must conclude that such use was often for reasons other than protecting the best interests of the children. Rather, denial of custody seemed to be leveled at the mother as punishment, perhaps because she dared violate social mores.

A further aspect of morality relates also to sexual behavior. A surefire way to lose custody is through evidence that adult sexual behavior occurred in the presence of the child; or worse yet, sexual behavior occurred between adults and children.

I worked with a family in which the mother had to prove that her child's coming into the mother's bedroom where the mother and a boyfriend were in bed nude together did not have a bad effect on the child. She eventually won custody, primarily because she proved that her ex-husband had allowed the children to witness him in bed with a girl friend, and that she had other qualities that would benefit the child.

In another example, the court gave custody to the father and cited the mother's "belief in the propriety of indulgence . . . in extramarital sex experimentation." And in another case, the testimony of two daughters (nine and fifteen years old) led to a mother's losing a custody dispute with the father, because the younger girl told of the mother's boyfriend entering the bed where she and her mother were sleeping and of sexual activities occurring between the two adults in her immediate presence.

To summarize, the court has no sympathy with liberal sexual views, and this seems to be an area where there is little room for debate. The position is that children must be safeguarded from sexual openness in general and that sexual behavior not condoned by society, such as sex outside of marriage, must not be endorsed. Parents are charged to "properly provide for and supervise the social and moral needs of the children."

Other Factors Relating to the Parents' Desire and Ability to Care for the Child

A review of law cases reveals other important factors related to what would presumably be the parents' desire and ability to care for the child. These include: "strength and sincerity of the desire for the child's custody; the ability of the claimant to care for the child as revealed by past performance; the remarriage of a claimant and the willingness of the new spouse to accept the child; the physical conditions in which the child is to live; and the mental health of the parties as it affects their ability to care for the child" (Clark, 1968, p. 586).

Financial resources, which are often thought by parents to be tantamount to validating their right to custody of their children, have been given little weight by the courts. The one exception seems to have been with fathers in very high-paying professions winning custody over mothers without a high professional status. This may have been, however, based on a rationale of status, as opposed to finances for supporting the child.

Courts have usually held that siblings (brothers and sisters) should not be separated. Exceptions to this guideline have typically been because the welfare of the children clearly required a different course of action. For example, I was involved in a case in which the parents of five young children (ages three to twelve) had been making commercial pornographic pictures—photos of the children from three families and their parents engaged in sex acts. When the court removed the children from the convicted parents' custody, it was concluded that the nature of their past family relationship supported that they should be placed individually in separate homes. That is, the court reasoned that the adverse effects of their involvement in the adult-child sexuality could best be counteracted by keeping them apart, at least for some time.

Jurisdiction also enters into this discussion of "other factors." Since I have dealt with this issue separately, I will merely repeat that plans to move to another state have been viewed negatively. Courts have often not approved the granting of custody to one parent when there were plans for one of them to move elsewhere, thereby uprooting the children and/or creating a situation where the children would be separated by a great distance from either parent.

In this age of mobility and jet travel, however, there seems to be a trend toward more liberal definition for this issue, as long as mutual visitation rights can be accommodated. For example, I consulted with one family in which the court had given the mother permission to move six hundred miles away from the father, but only after provisions (including cost and travel supervision) had been spelled out to assure that the ten-year-old boy would be able to spend as much time with his father as he did when they lived in the same state (which was only one weekend per month, since they lived over one hundred miles apart within the same state).

The Child's Wishes

Whom do you prefer to live with, Mommy or Daddy? That's the question that I suspect most parents consider asking their child when they sense a separation and/or divorce is imminent. Be advised, the child's answer may make less difference in the custody decision than you think or wish.

Before any consideration is given to the child's wishes, the court requires that the child must be old enough to form an intelligent judgment. If such intelligent judgment can be substantiated and if he or she is old enough, the wish or choice may be given significant weight.

The actual age the child must be for his or her views to be considered is not fixed. In other words, in some states the wishes of a young child will be considered, whereas in others the child might have to be at least a teenager. Generally speaking, most relevant statutes specify fourteen years of age as the point where a child's preference to be with a given parent should be considered.

A general guideline is that the younger the child, the less weight his or her preference will carry in the mind of the judge. Similarly, the preference of a child with limited intelligence, such as a mentally retarded child, regardless of age, would be given less consideration than the preference of a highly intelligent child (in the case of a handicapped child, however, there is reason to believe that ability to meet the special needs of that child, such as for rehabilitation services and constant care, would be of primary importance).

From my analysis of common-law cases, I believe there are four points. First, the child does not have a legal "right" *per se* to state a preference and have it counted in the judicial decision. The child's preference is viewed legally as a privilege. Second, the child must meet whatever the particular state defines as the "sufficient age" for his or her preference to be considered. Third, intelligence enters into the acceptance or rejection of the child's wish. Finally, if the life styles of the two parents are quite different and it is not clear-cut which parent could provide for the best interests of the child, the child's preference may be given weight in the decision-making.

The Race, Religion, and Social Views of the Parents

Race is a prominent social variable, but it has not proved to be an issue in enough custody cases to allow for generalizations about how it enters into the decision-making. About the only cases that demonstrate that race did, in fact, enter into the determinations are those where the parents were of different races and the child possessed external characteristics most like those of only one of the parents. For example, if the mother is Caucasian and the father is black and if the child has predominantly black facial features and skin coloration, there is reason to believe that the black father will have a strong chance of gaining custody, all other things being equal. Historically, the courts have accepted the concept for racially mixed children that the child with Negro blood and features is automatically considered black.

Religion presents a somewhat different situation. In many state custody acts, there is statutory reference to religion. Since the United States Constitution prevents the state from assisting or interfering with religious establishments and practices, religion has a dual status in child custody: on the one hand, it is identified as important to the best interests of the child, yet on the other hand it has played only a minor role in past custody disputes and decisions. To be candid, the sensitivity of the church/state relationship seems to result in religious issues being given the "kid-gloves" treatment in custody cases.

The basic question is whether religion will contribute beneficially to the child's development. While the court investigates religious views, it does not assume that a parent lacking religious convictions cannot be a moral, affectionate, successful mother or father. One noted legal analyst commented that "a reading of the cases leads to the conclusion that too many courts require lip service to a particular religious faith and a showing of some essentially meaningless religious observances as the price of obtaining custody" (Clark, 1968, p. 589).

Common law supports that the court does not attempt to discriminate between different religions. In other words, one denomination or religious doctrine is not viewed as superior to another one. On the other hand, the importance of regional and local social values and mores would support that a commonplace or orthodox religion would probably be viewed more favorably than some unusual religion that was considered "strange" by residents in that jurisdiction.

Probably the overriding relevance of religion is its significance as a factor in maintaining continuity for the child's life style. In other words, if the child has been brought up in a given religion, subsequent placement options will be evaluated, in part, on the basis of allowing continuation of the original religion. This was evident in a case where both the mother and father were killed in an accident. An aunt and uncle on the mother's side and an aunt and uncle on the father's side competed for custody of the children. Both couples seemed quite capable of adequately meeting the best interests of the children and providing them with a good home. The final decision was based on the fact that the mother and father had been from different religions, and the children were awarded to the aunt and uncle that practiced the same religion in which the children had been reared.

It seems noteworthy that some couples enter into agreements about rearing children in a certain religion before the children arrive or the marriage takes place (such as a premarital church-related "contract"). These special arrangements for bringing up a child in a particular religion have not controlled the decision-making in most cases.

Another unique circumstance appears when one parent is "highly religious" and the other parent professes little or no religious belief. There have been contradictory decisions on this matter. At this point in time, the issue of a religious parent versus an avowed atheist or agnostic parent remains inconclusive in terms of principles from common law.

Social behavior is difficult to evaluate objectively. The general social behavior of both parents is typically evaluated, usually from the point of view of the type of home environment that would be afforded to the child if custody placement were granted.

Child-custody decisions, contrary to what would be expected in a supposedly objective area, have often reflected consideration for social views. In a case in which there were negative factors about both the father and the mother, the court awarded the divorce to the father, but custody to the mother. However, it went on to regulate her social behavior in the interest of the children, specifying that any friends in either of their homes in the presence of the children could only be there "when it is for the social welfare of the children as distinguished from having social functions for the benefit of either" the mother or the father. Likewise, it is not uncommon for the court to specify that divorced parents may not entertain an "alleged paramour" in the home when the children are there. This has even been true in some cases where adultery had not been established.

When social factors become mixed, some interesting deliberations can occur. With a combination of religion, politics, and race, one case involved a maternal grandmother in a dispute with a mother for custody of a seven-year-old girl (the father had been killed in an accident). The grandmother alleged that the mother was a communist, was not raising the girl in her Jewish faith, had remarried to a black, and left the child in a day-care nursery too much. The court held for the mother, indicating that the factors the grandmother alleged did not constitute neglect. In general, the following pattern seems to prevail: if social factors are introduced, it is necessary to prove that the parent presumably possessing negative social factors would allow these factors to be detrimental to the welfare of the child.

It should be added that social factors are not always discounted. In a widely publicized battle between the maternal grandparents and the remarried father (the mother was deceased), the decision was for custody to the grandparents on the grounds that the father had an arty, bohemian life style, whereas the grandparents led a conservative, rural Midwestern existence. This case too suggests a guideline: courts have little sympathy for alternative life styles; they trust traditional family patterns.

The Effects of a Contract by the Parents Governing Custody

Beyond religious "contracts," parents have occasionally drawn up some sort of custody agreement, such as part of a separation pact. If the agreement should be scrutinized in a child-custody case, regular principles of contract law are applied. In other words, a judgment is made as to whether or not it is a valid contract.

Even if the agreements are deemed valid and/or worthy of consideration within the child-custody legal proceedings, the court can disregard them partially or totally. In these instances, they are discounted because there are other factors that are thought to be more important to the child's welfare.

The Putative Parent

A putative parent is the parent of an illegitimate child. The mother of an illegitimate child has typically been given custody if she wants—and without questions being raised about fitness to care for the child (unless the issue arises at a time other than at the birth, such as for child abuse later). But the social stigma of having an illegitimate child has led many an unwed mother to place the child for adoption or to seek an abortion.

There has been serious question as to whether the father of an illegitimate child is legally a parent. Since it is increasingly being held that the father must provide financial support to the illegitimate child, there is a strengthening view that the putative father does have a legal right to request custody or to obtain visitation rights.

From a legal point of view, the rights of the putative parent, be it the mother or the father (but especially the father), are unclear. The movement toward sexual equity under law and the prominence of the concept of the best interests of the child have combined to make it probable that putative parents will receive important new considerations in child custody. It seems quite feasible that the father of an illegitimate child could win custody if he could establish that he was better able than the mother to care for and raise the child.

Available Alternatives in the Framing of the Decree

The possibility of divided custody versus custody by only one of the parents poses a major question for the courts. This issue, obviously, ties into visitation rights. And there is a connection to the previously discussed matter of maintaining stability, such as by avoiding any uprooting of the child, as might occur if divided custody led to the child's being shifted from one state to another.

Divided or shared custody exists when one parent has the child for a specified period of time and then the child shifts to the other parent for a specified period of time. This kind of arrangement is well exemplified by one couple who, after their divorce, continued to live in separate houses in the same neighborhood (but more than walking distance apart). The custody decision placed the four-year-old girl and five-year-old boy with the mother for six months, after which time they packed their clothes and toys and moved to the father's house for the next six months, and then back again to the mother, and so on. Throughout each custody period, the other parent had generous visitation rights, thereby allowing for a minimal amount of separation from either parent, regardless of which house the children were residing in at the time. This is, however, one of those rare instances where the divorced couple maintained mutual respect for each other's rights after the divorce and cordial contacts when they encountered each other through the children.

Divided custody is generally avoided. It continues to be an important option because it is recognized that it is important for the child to have the opportunity to know and have affection for and from both parents.

Visitation rights are used most commonly to solve the above-mentioned problem. In other words, the child remains with one of the parents, and the other parent has a prescribed arrangement for spending time with the child. Perhaps the most widespread stereotype of visitation arrangements in the United States today would be that in which the mother receives the custody and the father is assigned the child for all or part of the weekends and school vacations.

It is essential that reality and the best interests of the child be kept in mind through negotiations about visitation rights. In thinking of families with which I have worked, I recall two examples of important points.

One remarried mother went to extremes to prevent the remarried father from having any visitation rights (she tried to get the court to reverse a previous decision that allowed him weekend contacts), apparently because of her deep-seated anger toward her ex-husband. In the name of righteously protecting her children, she was actually pursuing a neurotic motive—getting back at her husband—which held the potential of depriving her children of crucial contact with their father and jeopardizing her own mental health by allowing her to avoid constructively resolving her negative feelings toward her ex-husband and developing a healthier relationship with her present husband.

Another remarried mother also sought to get a court reversal on a decision giving her remarried ex-husband monthly out-of-state visitation rights. On inspection, it was determined that he had a history of very irrational behavior and had told relatives that he fully intended to brainwash the children into refusing to return to their mother after one of their visits or, if that failed, to forcibly keep them in the other state and try to get the custody case heard in a new jurisdiction. It all added up to a seriously disturbed father; the court had little difficulty in deciding that his visitation rights should be redefined to seeing the children only in their home town.

To repeat the obvious: when considering alternatives for custody and visitation rights, it is essential that the best interests of the child be foremost in your mind. You must not let your children become pawns in your unresolved and ongoing conflicts with your ex-spouse. This is one area where the opinions of experts on child development are essential. For example, astute analysis of the child's development and needs by a clinical social worker or personality assessment by a clinical psychologist can provide important data for deciding which custody or visitation option will be most beneficial for the child while still honoring the needs and rights of the parents.

8.

Choosing Your Weapons

In entering a custody battle, you obviously must know what weapons are in your arsenal. Stated differently, you need some notion as to what factors will be looked on with favor by the persons involved in the legal proceeding, both your allies (the experts you bring in to testify on your behalf) and your enemies (those experts whom your ex-spouse will rely upon).

The preceding chapter provided a rather thorough overview of the kinds of factors and illustrative cases that have influenced courts in the past. As I pointed out when defining common law, the American court system relies heavily on precedent cases, especially in domestic-law areas such as child custody.

Consequently, the common-law or precedent cases must be considered by you and your attorney when you begin formulating your strategy, and they will play an important role in this choosing-your-weapons phase of your planning. While a contemporary state child-custody statute might seemingly negate some of the reasoning that went into cases from another era, given the nature of man—a conditioned creature who relies upon past experiences and has trouble objectively approaching new situations, even with clear-cut new learning directions—it may be expected that common law will influence the legal proceedings in general and the judge's determination in particular.

In this chapter, I will assume that you and/or your attorney have reasoned through the relevance of the common law to your particular concerns and that your main task is to prepare your case for being deemed more suitable than your ex-spouse (or any other potential "psychological parent") to provide a home that will meet the best interests of your child.

The concept of the best interests of the child, as elaborated upon in Chapter 3, does predominate in statutory law today, and decisions based on this concept are rapidly eliminating incongruous precedents established in common or case law. Therefore, the material in this chapter focuses on the factors that are used by "experts"—such as lawyers, psychiatrists, psychologists, and social workers—to evaluate a parent for suitability for custody.

To give you some idea about the evolution of the views expressed in this chapter, I sifted through lawbooks analyzing child-custody cases and reviewed state statutes on child custody, and then made a list of what seemed to be the major factors. I then gave that list to a group of psychologists and social workers who had experience with child-custody court cases and asked them if there were some factors that were unimportant or if I had omitted any other important factors. Combining all of our ideas, I came up with a list of twenty factors that, when taken together, seem to represent the major factors in which a court would probably be interested if it were evaluating a parent's suitability for meeting the best interests of the child. These "top twenty" factors are:

1. AGE
2. ASPIRATIONS
3. CHILD-CARE HISTORY
4. CHILDREARING ATTITUDES
5. CRIMINAL RECORD
6. EDUCATION
7. GENERAL LIFE HISTORY
8. INCOME
9. INTELLIGENCE
10. KNOWLEDGE OF CHILD DEVELOPMENT
11. MENTAL HEALTH
12. MORALITY
13. PERSONAL BEHAVIOR
14. PERSONALITY
15. PHYSICAL HEALTH
16. QUALITY OF RELATIONSHIP WITH THE CHILD
17. RELIGION
18. SEXUAL BEHAVIOR
19. STABILITY OF RESIDENCE
20. VOCATION

Simply reviewing this list should suggest how each factor within a parent could contribute to or detract from meeting the best interests of the child.

A brief alphabetical listing such as this, however, does not indicate which are the most important factors. So as the second step, I sent this list to six hundred lawyers, psychiatrists, psychologists, and social workers (seventy-five males and seventy-five females in each of the four disciplines). I asked them to rank-order these twenty factors—in other words, to indicate which factor they thought was the most important for evaluating a parent, which would be the second most important, and so on until they reached the factor that was the least important. (Keep in mind that being least important does not mean it is *not* important. The past use of all of these factors in precedent cases and/or their being specified in state child-custody statutes make it evident that each of them could potentially be important.) Since I believed it important to ascertain whether these professionals thought any of the factors might be more important for the mother than the father, and vice versa, I asked them to make a separate rank-order listing for the mother and another rank-order listing for the father.

My research has shown that lawyers, psychiatrists, psychologists, and social workers do not make an overall distinction in the importance of these factors when applied to evaluating the mother as opposed to evaluating the father. The computer analysis of their rank-ordered ideas did reveal, however, that there were occasionally times when one of the four professional groups might believe that a mother should be evaluated differently than the father on a particular factor. I will present the findings on this issue in Chapter 10.

In the following pages, I will present the "top twenty" factors—not in alphabetical order this time, but in the order of importance. Since the order would be slightly different if we considered the factors according to the mother versus the father, I will present two lists at the end of the book that specify the order for the mother and father separately (see Appendices A and B). In this chapter, however, I will combine the information to provide the order for parents, regardless of their sex.

After each factor is presented, a brief discussion clarifies its meaning in practical terms. Since Chapter 10 will deal with choosing your allies (that is, picking professionals to help you present your case, such as by serving as expert witnesses on your behalf), I will end each section with a listing of the professional disciplines that could most likely contribute to evaluating the particular factor. The professional disciplines will be presented in the order of probable greatest contribution (but each listed would have the potential of making an important contribution). If you do not fully understand the differences between the professional disciplines, just keep in mind that Chapter 10 will elaborate on the disciplines (such as the difference between a psychiatrist and a psychologist) and will offer you guidelines for locating a professional to involve in your child-custody case. So as you read the listings of professional disciplines in this chapter, be aware that you may later want to refer back to these listings to better understand the relevance of a given professional discipline to a particular factor.

Now let us move on to the "top twenty" factors for evaluating parents for meeting the best interests of their child.

1. Quality of Relationship with the Child

The quality of relationship is a very broad factor and encompasses many of the other factors in the "top twenty" list. The major point is that professionals believe that the most important factor is an overall assessment of how the parent and the child get along. This would give consideration to communication, expression of affection, the sense of caring, and so on. There is heavy reliance on the psychological nature of the parent-child relationship. If the child is mature enough, it might be expected that this is a factor where the child's wishes (i.e., with which parent he or she would prefer to be placed) will be considered by the court.

Allies: Those who have needed specialized knowledge are child psychologists, child psychiatrists, marriage and family counselors, and family-oriented social workers (and perhaps any professional who has some expertise in human behavior and who has contact with the parent-child relationship, such as a minister or teacher).

2. Mental Health

Mental health is a touchy issue, but experts believe it is highly important to the welfare of the child. In fact, there have been court decisions that reflected a distrust for the parent with a history of mental problems, such as might have required psychiatric treatment. If you have had psychiatric treatment, you will need to counteract any stigma or negativism brought out.

It is important for you to distinguish between mental problems that reflect your longstanding personality characteristics and those that might have been brought on by a crisis. For example, I have found that many parents have received treatment in mental-health clinics (such as from a psychiatrist or psychologist) during the period when they were trying to keep their marriage together or were considering a divorce, and for all practical purposes the treatment was for problems brought on by the marital relationship. The fact that such treatment was sought can be used as a positive factor.

If you received psychiatric treatment because of the faulty marriage, it is a good strategy to present the treatment history as a plus on your side. In other words, you were the one who took the responsibility for trying to salvage the marriage and family for the benefit of everyone—your child and your ex-spouse included—and had the marital problems not existed (and everyone knows that you alone did not create the marital problems, because "it takes two to tango"), you would not have needed the treatment.

The most important point is to substantiate your current mental-health status. You should document that you are effective when coping with stress and that your support for the children is and will be stable.

Allies: Psychiatrists, clinical psychologists, clinical social workers, marriage and family counselors, any medical physician, and any professional with specialized training in clinical diagnosis and/or counseling and psychotherapy can evaluate the mental-health factor.

3. Childrearing Attitudes

Childrearing attitudes reflect knowledge of how a child develops and how a parent can best cultivate a healthy personality and appropriate behavior for the child. The way a parent disciplines is often focused upon. This is an area you could quickly remedy, should you think your ex-spouse might try to place emphasis on your ineptitude at raising a child. You can enroll in special courses designed to prepare you to be an effective parent (and maybe even bring the instructor in later as an expert witness on your behalf). You can volunteer to be an adult leader, such as a teacher's aide, for a children's program, such as helping out in a day-care program for preschoolers.

The important task is to document that you know what you are doing when you rear your children and that your personal characteristics (such as might be related to mental health) do not impede; to the contrary, emphasize how your characteristics accommodate wise childrearing.

Allies: Help may be gained from any professional who works with children, including child psychiatrists; child, school, and developmental psychologists; family-oriented social workers; marriage and family counselors; educators; and school guidance counselors.

4. Child-Care History

Child-care history (which tied with personal behavior in the professionals' rankings) is, as you might expect, simply an objective evaluation of how well the parent has met the best interests of the child in the past. It involves looking at all aspects of your relationship with the child, how you have conducted yourself in your general life style (such as making yourself available to spend time with the child), and your contribution to the quality of the home environment (such as providing good nutrition, careful supervision, and so on). If you have weaknesses in this area, it is critical that you take steps to be prepared to explain them (honestly and logically) to the court and that you have a well-thought-out plan for convincing the court that in the future you can and will provide the child with an improved existence.

Allies: Family-oriented social workers and any professional working with children can be called upon.

5. Personal Behavior

As mentioned, this factor actually tied for fourth place in the professionals' rankings. Personal behavior refers, in all candor, to how rational and productive your past and present behavior, broadly defined, seems to be.

Any episodes of reckless, irresponsible behavior on your part will be viewed negatively and must be faced in the manner described in the preceding section—namely, by having an honest and logical explanation and having a sound plan for improvements in the future. If these behaviors detracted from the child's welfare in any manner (such as episodic drinking that cost money, took you away from the home, and created an alcoholic state that could endanger the child), then there will be a definite negative reaction from the court. This is the kind of factor that you, of course, want to point toward in the evaluation of your ex-spouse. In other words, you want to promote a comparison of your past and present personal behavior with that of your ex-spouse, on the assumption that in the eyes of the court you will appear to be the better of the two. Be aware that "better" is strictly a societal definition. In other words, the court will make all evaluations according to the value system of society, as relevant to the best interests of the child. So if you or your ex-spouse have values different from those of society in general (such as believing children need to be self-determining, which results in the child's being on his or her own quite a bit), these will become ammunition, either for offensive or defensive purposes.

Allies: Any professional who can speak authoritatively about human behavior can contribute relevant information.

6. Physical Health

Physical health is viewed differently from mental health. Rightly or wrongly, emotional problems are often viewed as something people bring on themselves, whereas physical problems are viewed as being brought on by fate and beyond the control of the individual. Thus in child-custody deliberations, the parent's physical health will be given important consideration, but not from the point of view of discrediting the parent's overall qualities as a "fit person." Physical health will be evaluated for how it will affect the care of the child.

A good illustration is found in cases where a parent with a severe physical handicap—perhaps being blind or deaf—was still granted custody, as opposed to a nonhandicapped ex-spouse or a foster placement. The handicapped parent demonstrated to the court that his or her physical condition, while perhaps being a handicap, was of less importance than the love, care, and affection the parent could provide the child.

Allies: Any medical physician and other health-care specialists (e.g., nurses, physical therapists, etc.) who can assess the relevance of physical condition to ability to care for the child should be of assistance.

7. General Life History

General life history (which tied with personality in importance) is very similar to the parent's personal behavior (which ranked fifth), but encompasses every possible facet of life. Again, the important issue is how well the child's best interests have been met in the past and the probability of their being met in the future, as determined by the parent's general life style and pattern for living. Social values will play a large role in determining adequacy.

Allies: Any professional may offer evaluative material, with the choice depending upon the unique issues in your life history.

8. Personality

Personality, which tied for seventh place, relates to psychological characteristics, social skills, ability to get along with others, moods and emotions, and patterns of behavior that reflect personal adjustment. Obviously, mental problems, either through being present or absent, would be a reference point for determining personality.

Objective evidence, as opposed to opinions, is generally preferred, because it relies upon statistical comparisons of your personality factors with those of the general population. This necessitates taking personality tests. Probably the foremost personality tests for purposes of child custody are the Minnesota Multiphasic Personality Inventory, the Rorschach Ink-Blots Method, the Thematic Apperception Test, and the Sixteen Personality Factors Tests, but there are several hundred other tests that could be beneficial, including some directed at parenting factors.

Allies: Clinical psychologists, psychiatrists, and clinical social workers are most able to evaluate personality.

9. Morality

Since this factor received elaboration in Chapter 7, suffice it to say here that morality is determined by society, not by your personal definition. My research has revealed that professionals, whom one would expect to be fairly open-minded, tend to frown on unconventional definitions of morality (such as the so-called "new morality" with liberal attitudes toward sexual behavior) when the issue involves child custody. If you want to win custody, you must establish yourself as being impeccably moral. Of course, creating doubt about your ex-spouse's morality would strengthen your case. This is, however, one factor in which deficits on the parts of both natural parents could lead to a court decision to grant custody to someone else, such as a relative or a foster home.

Allies: You can call on essentially any professional, and religious workers (e.g., ministers, priests, and rabbis) and community leaders may also be useful.

10. Criminal Record

The criminal-record factor tied with intelligence in importance. By definition a crime is an affront to society. It can almost go without saying that a parent with a criminal record will usually be at a disadvantage in a custody dispute. While the nature of the crime has some relevance (presumably a one-time burglary offender would be less suspect than someone convicted, perhaps even just accused, of a violent crime or a sex offense), a criminal record could serve to disqualify a parent from custody. Exceptions would require a highly effective counteraction by expert testimony attesting that the future of the parent looks promising and the past would have no relevance.

Allies: Information from any professional is potentially worthwhile, but especially from criminologists, probation officers, psychiatrists, psychologists, social workers, court workers, and attorneys.

11. Intelligence

The intelligence of the parent, which tied for tenth place, is important only in terms of how it can restrict or enhance proper care for the child. Obviously, a significantly retarded individual would be less likely to be preferred for custody than a highly intelligent person, all things being equal. If, however, the difference is not marked, it is doubtful that a person who was somewhat "duller" than the other parent would be disqualified on these grounds; much more importance would be placed on, say, the quality of the relationship between the parent and the child. Intelligence is usually viewed in the same context as the education and vocation of the parent, so attention should be given to these factors when they are presented. If intelligence is to be a factor for consideration by the court, an individual intelligence test should be administered. The two foremost tests for this purpose are the Wechsler Adult Intelligence Scale and the Stanford-Binet Intelligence Scale.

Allies: Psychologists are best suited for evaluating intelligence.

12. Income

Many people have the idea that money can buy happiness. It is not unusual to find an argument that placement should be granted to a particular parent because that parent has the highest financial status and can, the assumption goes, provide the best for the child. With few exceptions, this has been proved to be a false notion.

Courts do not tend to place the parent's income very high on the list of factors for consideration. And this position is reflected in the fact that the professionals I contacted ranked it in twelfth place.

Financial status is considered, but only to the point of guaranteeing that the needs of the child can be met at an acceptable level. In other words, a reasonable income is needed for the child's welfare, but wealth or an above-average income is not seen as either necessary or as important as other considerations—such as a strong parent-child relationship, love, caring, and a stable home situation.

Allies: Most professionals can make some comment on the general relevance of income to the factors they will be evaluating. If income over a long range should be a critical factor because of the uniqueness of the case—say a child with a medical problem that may require expensive and extensive health and educational services for many years—perhaps a specialist in business, finance, or economics might be consulted.

13. Knowledge of Child Development

This factor is based on academic knowledge—how much do you really know about how and why a child develops the way he or she does? The underlying idea is that the more you can know, the more likely it is that you can help the child through expected developmental crises and promote healthy development.

This factor is very similar to the higher-ranked childrearing attitudes (third in importance). As mentioned in the discussion of that factor, you can take steps to remedy any lack of knowledge you may have about child development, such as by taking classes designed to promote effective parenting. You can also get involved with children's groups (in church or at a day-care program), read books, and do many other things that will allow you to introduce to the court the idea that you are well informed about the developmental needs of children, even if you may not have formal college training in the area.

I would urge you at this time to turn back to the section on childrearing attitudes and review the comments I made about that factor.

Allies: Any professional who works with children, as listed for the parent's childrearing attitudes, can evaluate your knowledge of child development.

14. Stability of Residence

Providing a stable residence for the child after a divorce has played a prominent role in many child-custody decisions. The decision has frequently reflected the desire to place the child in the same house where he or she has been living, the assumption being that continuing to live in the same residence will facilitate the child's adjustment to a one-parent family. Apparently, however, geographical stability is seen as a rather superficial condition, since the professionals in my research did not rank it higher. Distinct from simply placing the child in the same physical or geographical location, there is much more merit to basing the custody decision, in part, on the desirability of keeping the child in a home situation that has afforded psychological stability. If you will recall from Chapter 3, the Michigan Child Custody Act specified in its factors for evaluation: "Length of time lived in an emotionally or psychologically stable, satisfactory environment and the desirability of maintaining continuity." Then separately, it specified: "Permanence of proposed custodial home." The first factor obviously strives to evaluate the psychological health of the child's home life and to combine it with emotional stability by not disrupting the physical existence. This is in contrast to the second factor, which simply looks at the geographical fixity. The comprehensive concept, involving both the psychological and geographical considerations, has the most relevance to meeting the needs of the child, and this should play a prominent part in your custody planning.

Allies: Because of the comprehensive nature of the issues of permanence and continuity of residence, most professionals can contribute something to the evaluation of these matters, but the predominance of psychological concerns make it likely that psychologists, social workers, and psychiatrists, along with marriage and family counselors, could provide the most help.

15. Education

A parent's education is presumed to provide an index of two things: potential for maintaining financial stability in the home and knowledge of child development. My comments concerning childrearing attitudes, intelligence, income, and knowledge of child development combine to give a fairly thorough explanation of the importance of education.

Courts do not usually give much consideration to the actual grade completed by a parent or whether the parent holds a college degree, except as it might relate to keeping financial stability and having knowledge of child development.

If there is a large discrepancy between the parents—say a mother with only a high school education and a father with a doctor's degree—education might be considered, because of differences in life style that placement with a professional (such as the father) might offer to the child. Of course, this would still be of less importance, in most cases, than other psychological factors, such as the quality of the relationship between the child and each of the parents.

Like the parent's vocation factor—the last-ranked—

the education factor may be low in priority, but it does enter into cases, especially when one of the parents has attained professional prominence.

Allies: Any professionals versed in the relevance of education to income and childrearing, particularly psychologists and educators, can be contributors to your cause.

16. Aspirations

What a parent aspires to achieve could potentially bring benefits or detriments to the child. If the parent gains the accouterments of success, presumably the child will benefit through being able to enjoy those things that might serve his or her interests. If the parent had strong strivings that required time and energy, the child could easily suffer by being deprived of the parent's attention and care.

I have found that the parent's aspirations *per se* are not typically considered by the court to be particularly important in and of themselves. They become important only when placed in the framework of assuring benefits for the child.

Allies: Specialists in motivation, such as psychologists, are of key importance, but contributions can also be expected from other mental-health specialists, such as psychiatrists, social workers, and marriage and family counselors.

17. Age

The parent's age factor, which tied with the sexual behavior in importance, is generally viewed as being of little consequence, unless it suggests or is accompanied by health problems, difficulties in being employed, and similar factors that might jeopardize the welfare of the child. There are, of course, rare instances where one of the parents is very old (usually the father) or very young (usually the mother), and it is quite likely that age differences will be introduced as a reason why placement with a given parent should be preferred.

Allies: There is a new specialty of gerontology rapidly emerging in our society, and it might be well to seek out a psychologist with specialized knowledge of the aging processes. Otherwise, physicians, other health professionals, social workers, and family counselors could be consulted.

18. Sexual Behavior

The parent's sexual behavior tied for seventeenth place as a factor. It is ranked fairly low not because it does not carry strong impact when it is introduced, but because it is less common and less directly related to the prime consideration of meeting the best interests of the child.

As I mentioned in my discussion of morality, both earlier in this chapter and in Chapter 7, any sexual behavior by a parent that offends the mores of society will usually be viewed in child-custody proceedings as an indicator that the parent's suitability for custody is questionable. It seems clear that if the parent's sexual behavior has been in violation of the law or if the parent practices a sexual life style that would potentially be in the awareness of the child (such as what society would consider to be sexual promiscuity or deviance), it would be extremely difficult for the parent to keep custody, often even when other conditions are reasonably good (such as a fairly strong relationship between the parent and the child).

There have been few exceptions to this bias through the years, and when they have occurred (such as allowing a homosexual parent to retain custody), it seems that the decision has been based more on the lack of an available alternative placement than on anything else.

Allies: Psychiatrists, psychologists, social workers, physicians, family counselors, and religious leaders can be involved in evaluating sexual behavior; turn particularly to those who are Certified Sex Educators or Certified Sex Therapists by the American Association of Sex Educators, Counselors, and Therapists and Clinical Members of the American Association of Marriage and Family Counselors.

19. Religion

Despite the pronounced role that religion supposedly plays in our society, courts have tended to minimize consideration of this factor (which shares nineteenth position with the vocation factor). I discussed religion in detail in Chapter 7. The court will not: (1) distinguish one religion as being more desirable than another (except potentially in radical comparisons); (2) hold the lack of religion *per se* against a parent (as long as there is morality and caring present in the parent-child relationship); or (3) honor contracts created by a church (such as the Catholic Church's use of a prenuptial agreement that permits the marriage only if the child will be reared in the Catholic faith). On the other hand, the court will attempt to preserve religious consistency, if this seems to be part of the child's needed identity.

Allies: Avoid persons who would testify with religious zeal. The court wants only testimony that documents that the values and morals are helping the child, not that religion (or a particular doctrine therein) is essential for everyone. Reliance on professionals who integrate religion into a more comprehensive concept of child development is preferred. Thus, turn to psychiatrists, psychologists, social workers, marriage and family counselors, physicians, educators, and religious leaders.

20. Vocation

Tied for nineteenth place, the vocation factor typically takes a back seat to many other factors. It does, however, have the potential for being "frosting on the cake" in certain situations. I have alluded to the significance of one parent being exceptionally different from the other parent in income, intelligence, and education, and vocation can have the same kind of significance.

Reviewing common-law cases revealed to me that the vocation became a primary consideration when all else was equal and one of the parents was exceptionally high in vocational status, such as being a professional while the ex-spouse was unemployed. Likewise, if a child had long-term special needs (such as the example of the handicapped child needing medical services mentioned in the discussion of income), the vocational factor could enter into assessing the financial picture for the child's welfare.

I regret to report that I have uncovered a few child-custody cases where it looked as though there was discrimination against a nonprofessional parent in favor of a professional parent, strictly (or at least primarily) because of the professional parent's prominence in the community. Professionals from medicine and law seem to have received this privilege the most. The high status of a vocation seemed to carry significant weight for the father, especially if the mother could be proved to have engaged in any conduct (such as infidelity) that detracted from the high community status to which the child was entitled.

This factor could prove to be a powerful weapon for the high-status professional. The nonprofessional contesting against a professional ex-spouse had best be prepared to defend against a court's tendency to view elevated professional status as a source of contribution to the best interests of the child.

Allies: If you are on the defensive, choose a high-status professional (or several) from the same profession as your ex-spouse to denounce the importance of the profession for benefiting the child; if you are on the offensive, reverse the tactic.

9.
Being Prepared: Strategy, Not Fury

THE SOMEWHAT ACADEMIC INFORMATION presented in the foregoing chapters was intended to give you the background you need to have a reasonable chance of coming out a victor in a custody battle.

Since the time between divorce and a custody battle might be characterized as a cease-fire period or a lull before the storm, I would like to take a brief respite from the academic perspective to concentrate on the personal side of preparing to enter into child-custody legal proceedings. All the while, of course, the academic issues remain prerequisites for effective battling for custody.

I am reminded of how certain Indian warriors supposedly abstained from sexual relations before entering battle, in the belief that a sexual orgasm would sap their strength. While there seems to be no reason to believe that sexual abstinence will, in fact, preserve strength, the principle of preserving strength for the custody battle merits attention.

As another analogy, warriors from many cultures often prepared for battles in a ceremonial fashion, such as by taking a sauna, using switches to stimulate the skin, being massaged, and slowly and artistically girding for battle. Here, too, there are principles for child custody. First, as reflected in the warriors' attention to their bodies, it is essential to have the total organism functioning as fully as possible. Second, the mind must be honed to permit an effective mental state, one that allows keen perception and responses.

In this chapter, I will offer some ideas about how you can attain a strong personal set, one which preserves and builds ego strength and which promotes an integration of mind and body in such a manner as to maximize your performance and functioning when under fire in the custody proceedings.

They Can't Kick Sand in Your Eyes!

As a boy growing up, I was always intrigued by the advertisements in comic books for muscle-building systems. The bully on the beach raced by leaving a flurry of sand. The girl friend urged the ninety-seven-pound weakling into action, but he hesitated because of the strength of the bully. But after getting his Herculean muscles by mail-order miracle, he approached the bully and: POW!

While physical hostility has no place in a sane society (or a sane person), it will certainly help your chances of winning a custody battle if you go into the fray with all possible strength. In fact, the time of separation through the divorce to the custody proceedings is a good period both to preserve your optimum strength and to cultivate new "muscles."

The key lies in ego strength. Without a complex definition of how the ego develops and is maintained, let me simply say that ego strength refers to the degree of confidence, security, identity, self-understanding, coping behaviors, and defense mechanisms that a person is able to bring into threatening situations or instances in which decision-making or stress resolution must be effective.

Ego strength is no sudden acquisition. It takes us our whole lives, but particularly our childhoods, for setting up the ego structures and building the reservoir of defenses and strength. Thus, as an adult you must accept your developed status and be content to find ways to avoid wasting your resources, to cultivate more effective coping mechanisms (ways of behaving or responding), to get rid of ineffective or self-defeating (e.g., neurotic) defenses, and to acquire new sources of positive reinforcement (which will give you additional strength). Your basic personality structure will not change overnight. Would that personality change were as simple as the muscle development supposedly available by mail order! You can, however, preserve, refine, and improve yourself, and sometimes in pretty short order.

Wasting resources is an unnecessary expenditure of your energy. Probably worry and depression are the best examples of how self-defeating emotions or behaviors can waste valuable psychological resources. By engaging in self-pity or unjustified grief or anxious thoughts, you can quickly drain away exactly the qualities that could help you gain what it is you are lamenting, namely happiness and fulfillment.

Cultivating more effective coping mechanisms means learning how you can best avoid self-defeating emotions and behaviors and can exist free from disruptions. Placing the blame on others, refusing to admit to reality, developing psychosomatic complaints, and being constricted in reactions to others are just a few of the poor coping mechanisms or faulty ego defense mechanisms that you want to get rid of in your search for improved ways of behaving or responding.

While it sometimes takes much self-analysis (or professional psychotherapy) to gain a reasonably thorough understanding of defense and coping mechanisms or behaviors, it should be obvious that responses should be tailored toward self-respect and confidence, realistic perception, logical reasoning, and healthy attitudes and interests. As you might expect, being honest about yourself and others (instead of entertaining delusions about capabilities or handicaps), being realistic about what the present and future have in store (instead of avoiding responsibilities), and turning to others in a mutually beneficial manner (instead of pursuing some neurotic dependency or withdrawal) can be good avenues to a better life.

New sources of positive reinforcement are of special importance to the person who has just gone through a divorce and/or is faced with a custody battle. More will be said about this matter when I talk shortly about working for a healthy physical and mental state. Moreover, positive reinforcement can come from a number of activities I have touched on in previous chapters, such as just being involved in any activity (remember the research I mentioned about how occupational therapy counteracted depression as well as or better than psychotherapy?), entering into social relations, and having appropriate dating and sexual behavior.

In raising the issue of "reinforcement," I can move

toward an explanation of overall "ego strength." Persons familiar with personality theories and psychotherapeutic approaches will recognize that, in many ways, these two terms are incompatible—at least they were developed by professionals with quite different theoretical beliefs. As I have elaborated upon in detail in my book *Psychobehavioral Counseling and Therapy*, there is no reason to think that it is not theoretically possible and, indeed, practical for the most efficacious treatment to seek to integrate the conditioning-oriented principles associated with "reinforcement" into (or with) the psychodynamically oriented concept of "ego strength."

Reinforcement involves recognizing that when a specific kind of behavior occurs, the consequence of that behavior will influence whether it does or does not tend to occur again (or in some modified version). If a person does something—say, asserts a belief that would have previously not been admitted—the way the other person reacts will lead the assertive person to either sense that it is all right to be assertive or that it is not all right or that it might be all right if it were in a slightly different form. For example, if the second person responded to hearing the asserted belief with rejection, saying, "That's an idiotic idea, there is no way I'm going to listen to nonsense like that!" the first person would be apt to respond the next time (because of the evoked negativism) by cautiously admitting the belief (to another person) or keeping the belief unadmitted. On the other hand, if the second person, upon hearing the belief, said, "Hey, that's a swell idea. I wish more people believed the way you do!" or maybe less positively, "I don't really agree with you, but I certainly respect your right to say it and I admire your ability to come right out with your beliefs," the person would have received positive reinforcement and would be apt to repeat the act (that is, to be assertive in beliefs to others) in the future.

While I know many people think that negative responses are more powerful than positive responses, research has not substantiated that. Positive responses have much more power to increase a kind of behavior than negative responses have to extinguish a kind of behavior. This is an important principle for the person in the "cease-fire period" to keep in mind: if you wish to build your reserves or resources, you should set about finding ways to gain positive rewards or reinforcers.

This principle applies particularly to social relations, even the most casual contacts with others. That is, you usually have "ego invested" in any interactions with another person, though some are far more important than others. A series of aloof, rejecting comments, say from casual contacts with a series of salespersons in a shopping mall, can produce a negative reaction, such as self-doubt or anxiety or depression. On the contrary, a similar series of casual contacts with persons, accomplished in a way that will win you acceptance at the least and praise at best, can lead to good responses, such as feeling secure and happy.

The challenge, especially in the period of time when you may be under fire and somewhat drained of ego strength, is to pattern your life so that you purposefully avoid coming in contact with people who have something to gain by attacking or rejecting you. Instead, you should enter situations in which you at least have a fair chance of being accepted as you are and, you hope, going the step further to being liked.

You should particularly guard against self-defeating behaviors—in other words, situations where you are bound to come out on the short end of the stick. An example of self-defeating behavior would be the case I cited earlier of the female psychologist who met only undesirable males, yet continued to seek to meet men in a bar. Other examples would be excessive eating or alcohol consumption used to relieve anxiety with the result being, in the long run, increased anxiety and other negative effects.

Longtime friends and even relatives, while having the potential of being valuable assets at a time of stress, can also be liabilities. In friendships and family relations, it is rightly expected that there will be mutual benefits from the relationships. Unfortunately, many (if not all) people have a "crazy streak" or, more appropriately stated, neurotic needs. In other words, they have some illogical or unhealthy motive to produce a certain equally unhealthy reaction, frequently at another person's expense. Thus the person just through a divorce may be a prime target for psychological abuse from other people intent on fulfilling their own neurotic needs. Even family and friends are not exempt from this deleterious possibility. You must, therefore, enter all relationships, even those that you have had since birth, with a great deal of caution. You must not become a psychological punching bag for anyone. While this is healthy advice for any point in your life, it is especially critical at times of stress when you are in a "weakened ego state."

"Weakened ego state" may sound like psychological mumbo-jumbo, but it is an important reality, a condition that has to be recognized and counteracted by those going through divorce and child-custody legal proceedings. The stress and related insecurities and uncertainties combine to weaken one's defenses and sap away much-needed reserve psychological power.

Explaining the "ego" is probably one of the most complex problems in psychology. It is not a simple concept. It is not a concrete entity that can be specified and measured, and there is much disagreement even about its most basic definition and fundamentals.

In a sense, the "ego" is you. It is you as a psychological entity, and it develops from literally your first few seconds of life on to the present (from some of the recent treatises of life after death, perhaps it continues to develop beyond life as we know it!). It is composed of heredity and everything you learn and experience thereafter. It is your psychological organization, your capabilities—intelligence, personality, needs, defenses, drives, power—to live. It is a mediator of the good and the bad in your drive and need systems and your morals and values, and it sends this mediated message to your brain to determine how you should feel, act, behave, and respond.

Based on a psychoanalytically oriented model, the ego can be conceived as having only a set amount of strength (or fuel) for coping with life. Whenever you engage in problem-solving, such as worrying about something or interacting with someone who requires that you be on your toes, you are using your psychic strength. The reinforcement sources in your life, such as friends, work accomplishments, self-satisfaction, or children (which create a sense of self-worth and fulfill your altruism and nurturance needs), give you support and regenerate your resources.

Consequently, if you have only so much ego strength, it is apparent that the demands in your life could feasibly be so great, could require so much power to counteract, that your "energy reserves" (to use a popular phrase of the day) can become depleted.

When energy depletion occurs, the outcome is predictable: you are ineffective. You cannot cope with the most basic of life's tasks. The individual in this state finds little to be happy about and is thrust into a psychological condition in which insecurity, disappointment, guilt, depression, and self-destructive behaviors can readily take over.

To make sure that the stress of divorce and the child-custody legal proceedings do not deplete your psychological reserves—that is, do not reduce your ego strength to a level that will interfere with your functioning, to the jeopardy of yourself and your children—you must use this cease-fire period as a time to conserve energy and stock up the reserves.

These ideas about depletion of psychological reserves and the need for ego strength, combined with the comments throughout this book about the emotional and behavioral reactions commonly found among adults and children after divorce, have received considerable research attention for close to a century, and there has been extensive theorizing about how and why all of these emotional and behavioral reactions occur. While there is still debate, psychoanalytic theory seems to provide one of the most meaningful explanations.

My analysis of what happens prior to, during, and immediately after a divorce seems compatible with the psychoanalytic notions about so-called "traumatic neurosis." In his classic text *The Psychoanalytic Theory of Neurosis,* Otto Fenichel states: "All neurotic phenomena are based on insufficiencies of the normal control apparatus" (note that the ego is the primary "control apparatus"). As he describes the different ways that insufficiencies occur, Fenichel gives a basic definition, saying that "too much excitation enters the mental apparatus in a given unit of time and cannot be mastered; such experiences are called traumatic" (Fenichel, 1945, p. 19).

As I look at the effects of divorce, be they for adults or children, I believe there is evidence of three things. First, the person has a given amount of ego strength, which depends to a large extent on overall life patterns (for example, how the personality has developed and how able the individual is to receive reinforcements). Second, the events associated with the divorce send forth extensive stimuli which lead to excitation of the organism (or the person). Third and finally, the amount of time (coupled with the basic personality and/or ego strength) influences whether the excitation can be handled or whether it floods the organism. The relationship of these ideas to Fenichel's psychoanalytic explanation of a traumatic neurosis seems self-evident.

While I touched on the important symptoms in Chapter 4, four symptoms of traumatic neuroses derived from Fenichel's psychoanalytic theory should be acknowledged.

First, there is a "blocking of or decrease in various ego functions," which stated simply means that the person is less able than usual to exercise mental (and, in some cases, physical) capacities. An example would be that the person involved in a divorce may be less astute intellectually and less logical in problem-solving than he or she usually is.

Second, there is a proneness toward "spells of uncontrollable emotions, especially of anxiety and frequently of rage, occasionally even convulsive attacks." Clearly this means that the overwhelming excitation, for some persons, will result in emotional reactions that are not really part of the everyday pattern of behavior. The stress of divorce is likely to provoke such emotions.

Third, there may be "sleeplessness or severe disturbances of sleep with typical dreams in which the trauma is experienced again and again." It is anxiety that disrupts regular sleeping behavior, and it would not be uncommon for a divorcing person to dream a lot (as well as daydream) about the events of the past marriage or possible events of the future (particularly feared events).

Fourth, there can be "psychoneurotic secondary complications," which can essentially be almost any kind of problem emotional condition or behavior act that was formerly not common to the person and that erupts at the time of divorce as a source of adjustment difficulty. Among other things, this could include certain physical reactions (such as migraine headaches, chronic upset stomach, constipation, etc.) or emotional responses (such as irritability, depression, suspiciousness, boredom, etc.).

Psychoanalytic research reveals that persons experiencing a traumatic neurosis are prone to seek "secondary gains" from their problems. Essentially, this process entails seeking and getting rewards for "being sick." I strongly caution you against talking too freely about your problems or developing relationships that put you into a highly dependent role, because these actions can easily lead to your receiving reinforcement for being sick. This you do not need and must avoid. You need to work consistently to regain confidence and to engage in responsible actions.

Persons experiencing traumatic neurosis typically respond quickly to professional psychotherapy, especially if they led reasonably effective lives before the stressful situations developed. The prognosis is, of course, less optimistic for persons who previously were marginally adjusted or who have a history of emotional or behavioral problems.

It would be outside the scope of this discussion to go

into detail about therapeutic treatment of traumatic neurosis, but since there are some principles in the therapeutic procedures that might allow for self-implementation, let me note the primary techniques.

Getting distance from the persons, situations, or conditions that provoked the stress is fundamental. Rest and avoidance of more stress allows the person to collect energy, so to speak, for mastering the problems at a later date. Distancing and rest help the person reactivate the ego functions, such as intellect and logic, to the original pre-trauma condition, and provide the person with an opportunity to reestablish psychological equilibrium. This is called the "quieting-down" method.

Belated discharge of actions or emotions can be beneficial, but can also be painful (thus a professional therapist is often needed). With this approach, the person who withheld certain reactions during the stressful period, because expressing them would have led to psychological collapse or other detrimental effects, finally lets them all out. For example, the person who kept tight control on his or her disappointment, frustration, and anger during the divorce may need to get these feelings out of the system once the divorce decree has been granted. Obviously, one has to be careful how this belated discharge is allowed to occur and in whose presence. This is called the "stormy" method.

Catharsis—talking to ventilate feelings about the traumatic events—can be constructive, but as mentioned, secondary gains must be avoided. Working with a professional at this time may involve catharsis, a degree of passivity and dependence, and receiving honest reassurance and suggestions to "take it easy." Since there are some pitfalls to openness and dependence, it is apparent that professionals who are aware of the pitfalls will probably be more helpful than family or friends.

As this traumatic-neurosis model reveals, the effects of divorce are painful and, to many, devastating. Since for many people the divorce signals the termination of a substantial portion of one's life, a grief reaction is to be expected.

In addition to avoiding secondary gains, recovering from grief necessitates recognizing that the marriage, while over, has meaning for the present and future and that a direct replacement or substitute is unattainable. There may be contradictory impulses of trying to return to the past and trying to forget it forever. Either of these options would be foolish, since the past is gone and to deny the marriage would be avoiding reality.

It should be acknowledged that the grief reaction is not for the marriage, but for the psychological impact. In his book *Loss and Change,* Peter Marris captures the nature of the matter:

> If, as in divorce, the rupture may have been sought, it is not so much the lost relationship itself whose meaning needs to be retrieved, as the hopes and purposes it betrayed. The working out of grief is then a restoration of faith that such hopes are not futile; that one is not, after all, incapable of giving or receiving love. (Marris, 1975, p. 164.)

The "restoration of faith" requires the cultivation of ego strength.

Ego strength can be thought of as the source of energy, with the ego being the coordinator of the distribution of resources. To continue with the energy analogy, there are two primary generators for the energy: the organism and the mind.

The organism is the total system with all of the living parts. You might think of it mainly as the body, with all of its physiological complexity of functioning systems, but it includes psychological functioning as well. Since the mind will receive separate consideration, let us focus now on the physiological: the body.

Recall that the reason for this discussion is to help you maintain your strength to counteract the stress and adverse effects associated with separation, divorce, and child-custody legal proceedings. The motive is clear and simple: self-preservation for both you and your child. If your body is in less than peak condition, it could prove to be like the powerful race car that has to drop out or comes in behind the rest because of a malfunction in one part of the power system. In other words, your total functioning, regardless of your overall strength and fortitude, is dependent to a significant degree on your body not letting you down.

In this book I cannot go into great detail about why you need to keep a healthy body and how you can do it, but perhaps three concisely stated guidelines can serve our purpose.

1. Your diet must be controlled. Aside from any concern about gaining and losing weight for the sake of appearance, proper diet is essential for nutritional and metabolic reasons. Periods of stress, as a divorce might well be for most people, are known to have the potential of disrupting eating patterns; people either eat too little or too much. You should be sure that, even if your impulse is to skip meals or to overeat, you maintain proper eating patterns.

2. Your tension can lead you toward self-destructive acts. You should be on guard against this possibility. You should studiously avoid overindulgence in anything that

becomes a "neurotic crutch." Among many things, this could include being a glutton for junk foods, smoking excessively (of course, scientific research indicates that any smoking is excessive, since it is known to be destructive), and relying on drugs. Alcohol and "nerve medicines," such as tranquilizers, can be pitfalls at this time in your life, even if prescribed by a physician. Using any substance, such as alcohol or tranquilizers, to control tension is, except in rare instances, an attempt by the individual to avoid the responsibility of confronting the pressures of reality and beginning to solve problems. These substances prove to be only crutches and at some point they must be given up. If the person has not learned in the meantime to walk upright alone—that is, to use responsible judgment and to act wisely—he or she will collapse. So rather than relying on any substance for continual support, the healthy approach is to use these substances very cautiously, such as only under medical supervision and only for very brief periods, and *concurrently* to be engaged in activities that will eliminate the need for any kind of crutch. Counseling or psychotherapy is probably the best way to learn how to cope with the stress associated with reality and to develop new ways of feeling, acting, and behaving. Even though it is tempting to find relief through alcohol and drugs, you must remember two things. First, the relief will only be temporary; you will at some point have to be on your own anyway, so why not start strengthening yourself for the inevitable task now? Second, crutches are for the handicapped, and your quest for a fulfilling life, not to mention winning custody of your children, necessitates your being as fully functioning an individual as possible.

3. Exercise is important. It may be difficult to force yourself, but the organism demands exercise. This is a

need that goes beyond mere weight control or muscle building. And it must involve more than jogging around the block or touching your toes a dozen times. It is cultivating a state of mind that helps your body become a smoothly operating organism. People who have become able to jog several miles without stopping often report that their minds work on things other than the labor of running. To be sure, it is a form of meditation, a state of mind that voids tension. This kind of mind-body functioning can be encouraged by engaging in essentially any activity that seems potentially relaxing or enjoyable to you, particularly if physical movement is involved. But it is up to you to take the time to do it and to be responsible enough actually to enter into the activity. As I have mentioned several times, activity itself is healthful, and inactivity is destructive. The health of the organism depends on exercise, and only you can ensure that your organism gets enough of it.

These guidelines may sound like a physical-fitness lecture, but the intention is to emphasize more than physical stamina or athletic prowess. Most basically, the value of cultivating a healthy body is that it, in turn, can contribute to a healthy mind (which I will discuss shortly).

A healthy state is a dimension of the major "test" that a judge in child-custody legal proceedings administers when considering the evaluations of the mother and father for suitability for custody: the "fitness test." The fitness test is simply weighing the assets and liabilities of each parent to determine if each is fit to have custody, and, if so, which is more fit (or able) to meet the best interests of the child. Consequently, your efforts to achieve and maintain a healthy organism, as well as a strong state of mind, are directly attached (literally and figuratively) to the foremost objective of the child-custody determination: passing the fitness test.

Throughout, this book has touched upon your state of mind or your mental condition. Fundamentally, the issue is whether your personality, as developed through the years, can survive the pressures and stresses of a bad marriage and equip you to give your child (if you are granted custody) the psychological conditions necessary to be happy and healthy.

Again, in this book I cannot go into great detail about psychological factors, but there are five guidelines that anyone moving through the separation-divorce-custody series should follow:

1. Insight is essential. Even though it may have been a bad marriage, analysis of your relationship with your ex-spouse, as well as relations with others (family, friends, lovers, children), can prove helpful for finding ways to improve the present and the future. Insight can be gained on your own, or you may wish to involve a professional counselor or therapist. It is through insight that you learn why you did things, what opportunities are open to you, and how to solve present problems and avoid creating unnecessary new ones.

2. Options for improving your life need to be defined, carefully evaluated, tried out, and selectively retained in your life style.

3. As mentioned before, you should avoid situations or people that are apt to reactivate old conflicts or create new problems.

4. You should turn to other people in a healthy manner. Whenever you start to get involved with someone, including family and friends with whom you have had a long relationship, you should assess whether it is in your

best interest and whether the interaction will be a healthy one. Do not let neurotic needs or impulsive behavior lead you into involvements that will have negative effects.

5. In taking on new tasks or jobs, be sure they are attainable. In other words, do not try to do something that is beyond your ability. For example, I have noticed that some women immediately after a divorce start to work, presumably on the grounds that they need an income but actually because they think work will keep their mind off of their problems. That is, their motive is beyond real economic considerations. All too often, what happens is that they assume new responsibilities to add to a life that is already burdened, and there is no way they can satisfy all the demands being placed on them, especially in this period when their ego strength is sapped anyway. Thus they do not do well in their jobs and this failure sets them back psychologically, such as by decreasing their self-confidence. Or the work takes them away from their children, just when they and the children need the parental contact the most. Another example is the parent who comes out of a marriage and says, "I should go back to school," and enrolls for a full load of college courses. Again, the intention on the surface—to improve one's skills and to open up new employment possibilities—is constructive, but meeting the requirements of college courses creates new demands at a time when usually the last thing needed is more demands.

In no way are these five guidelines a complete program for strengthening your mental set. In fact, they are examples of but a few ways to avoid decreasing existing ego strength.

Finding methods to generate ego strength is a highly individualized process. Insight, as mentioned, allows you to assess options. Finding energy resources, whether petroleum or psychological strength, requires prospecting. In other words, you need to search out sources that can energize you in your own unique fashion. Understanding your need system and recognizing opportunities that are and are not available to you is the basic challenge. Much of this effort is self-generated, but the help of a professional may boost your chances for effective development of new ego strength.

The next chapter will describe various professionals who can assist you both in child-custody legal proceedings and in getting your life style in order. In this section on creating a strong strategy and a healthy mind-body state for ego strength, there are two guidelines for dealing with professionals that should complement the guidelines already listed:

1. While professionals have expertise and may be of a higher status than you because of advanced education or greater income, it is essential that you approach them with self-respect. Philosophically, all persons are equal, so you should consider yourself and the professional as equal in humanistic importance. But more specifically, the professional's expertise is simply that—acquired expert knowledge and skill. It does not make the professional an exceptional person in a complete fashion, certainly not in a manner that would depreciate your own worth. All of this is a way of saying that your welfare requires that you view professionals realistically, and for what they can and cannot bring into your life. They do not possess messianic qualities, they are not superhuman, and they are not necessarily prototypes of how to live. They are sources of consultation (which I will elaborate upon in the next chapter). Instead of standing in awe of the professional, you must scrutinize the wisdom, in a practical way, that underlies any counsel you receive.

Sometimes we tend to accept advice according to the status of the individual. That is, the more prominent or successful or the better-credentialed the person, the more powerful is his or her advice and the more apt we are to accept it. Certainly there are professionals whose prominence, success, credentials, and degrees are correlated to the wisdom of their advice, and these authorities should be highly valued. But there are others who may have the accouterments of wisdom but who, in point of fact, are not solid authorities. A rule of thumb would be: the higher the status of the professional, the more carefully you should scrutinize the advice for wisdom. Incidentally, mature and able professionals guard against their own tendencies toward defensiveness. This means that if any professional resists your inquiries (such as about credentials), you should suspect his or her authority. Secure professionals, regardless of discipline, are usually quite willing to justify their reasoning—and these justifications should be based on facts and research, not simply on statements such as "That's the way I know it should be done." So, through all dealings with a professional, your self-worth must be maintained, or else you remain especially vulnerable to depending on others and letting them make decisions for you.

2. Relationships with professionals should be objective and platonic. You are not buying a friend. You are employing a consultant with expertise to be made available on your behalf. Since professionals do operate in an authoritative manner and since you may well be flagging in ego strength, it may be tempting to rely too much on them. Certainly you should rely on their authority, but you must not rely on their personal selves. To become overly reliant on a professional in a regressive, neurotically dependent manner will not speak well for you in the

custody proceedings. And in the long run, it will not be constructive for you if you do not consistently move toward stronger, more autonomous functioning in the future.

More will be said in the next chapter about the professionals who can be involved in the child-custody determinations. These two guidelines, however, should alert you to certain considerations relevant to your quest for ego strength.

Mapping a strategy involves analysis of all critical factors. Most basically, it necessitates identifying the factors relevant to a custody decision. Given that human nature is subjective, there will probably be certain factors that you would rather overlook or minimize in importance. This tendency makes it all the more important to strive for objectivity. The use of professionals is the surest way to guarantee that you are accurate, objective, and honest about what factors are relevant to the custody determinations and what their true nature is. These are evaluation issues, so the strategy formulation will require professional consultation. Since the next chapter is devoted to professional consultation, I will defer extensive elaboration for the time being. But there are some related practical ideas I would like to offer.

You must identify and weigh every factor in your case, whether it relates to your own characteristics or those of your ex-spouse or those of your children, with an open mind. Moreover, you must be prepared, after you receive consultation, to change your views. For example, you must be willing to admit to certain deficits in yourself or strengths in your ex-spouse.

You must guard against vindictive motives creeping into your thinking. You must not be willing to combine opportunity for vengeance against your ex-spouse with your quest for custody. I have witnessed individuals engulfed in such an "I'll get even with that bastard" motive many times, and am convinced that such people are only following a destructive path. Such a motive is not only unrealistic and psychologically unhealthy (reflecting a poor personality composite on the part of the parent), but it holds the potential of long-range negative effects for both parent and children. There are only two ways to view custody. First, it is the fulfillment of a duty to the child, as defined by society. But this is not all. Second, and also of great importance, it is a matter of the parent's finding self-fulfillment through caring for his or her children.

As your consultants will constantly warn you, this cease-fire period is a time when you must avoid getting into any compromising situations with anyone, particularly your ex-spouse, family (watch out for in-laws!), and friends. You must accept once and for all that the divorce is final, that the marriage is over, and that you are now responsible for charting the future by planning.

Your planning for the future necessitates being a systems analyst. While your consultants will train you in this approach, the idea is that you have to analyze your life space and patterns to learn "what leads to what." In other words, if you act a certain way, what will be the results? You then trace all connectors—what act causes what response, and when that happens what will follow next, and when that occurs what can be expected, and so on through the chain of interacting factors—until you understand the systems (the patterns for the interacting factors) in your life. This systems analysis will allow you to plan your case for the custody proceedings and it will also give you valuable information for planning your personal life.

Being Prepared: Strategy, Not Fury

The foregoing comments place emphasis on the future, and this is of critical significance. Research has shown that people who live in the past are less healthy psychologically than those who live in the present and realistically plan for the future. I should hasten to add that those who cannot accept the present and who live only for the future are usually less healthy psychologically (like those who live in the past) than those people who are oriented to the present.

This point has special relevance to the individual during the period just after a divorce. It is easy and normal to be sucked back into the past, remembering all the dear moments or the fond memories, and this can only lead to distorting the past—making it better than it really was and shutting out the negative conditions that led to divorce. To do so will restrict your chances of making the most of the present.

While easier said than done (as is true with so many aspects of controlling human behavior), your goal should be to maximize the present and to realistically plan for the future. You can promote much of this "be here now" or present-oriented life yourself, but counselors and therapists can also help you in accepting that the past is over (and in learning from the experiences it contained), in planning for the future, and, above all, in making the present the best possible under the terms of the reality.

As a final concept for this cease-fire period, you should guard against becoming too egocentric. Protecting your best interests and fulfilling your needs in a healthy fashion is important, but it is a time when your parental responsibilities must also be at the forefront. Your children, of course, will experience many of the same pressures you will experience, and they need you just as you need them.

While you will also be a "self-advocate" in the child-custody proceedings, it is important that you be primarily a "family advocate." In addition to working for conditions that will benefit you and your children on an individual basis, you must also strive to attain conditions that will allow the family unit to be strengthened. For example, while you might want to shut your ex-spouse out of your life as much as possible and therefore be tempted to try to eliminate any visitation rights for him or her, the welfare of the children as individuals and consequently the strength of the family unit might benefit from the ex-spouse having contact with the children.

There are no clear-cut guidelines for strengthening the family unit in this crisis period. It is, I believe, more of an outlook on life that you should adopt. I think I captured the essence of the challenge a few sentences back: you must not be too egocentric. The child-custody determination is a mandate for a "family identity" for all concerned.

10.
Recruiting Allies

HAVING LEARNED the factors on which child-custody determinations are based and having taken the initial steps toward a strategy, you are now ready to recruit allies for the custody battle.

Your allies might include friends and family who can testify about your characteristics, the relationship between you and your child, and your fitness to provide your child with the right kind of upbringing. The court values these kinds of information from family and friends, but it tends to put greater value on the expert opinions of professionals.

Professionals involved in child-custody cases include attorneys, psychiatrists, other medical physicians (especially family practitioners and pediatricians), psychologists (especially clinical and child psychologists), other behavioral scientists (especially sociologists), social workers, marriage and family counselors, educators, and (to a lesser extent) religious and community leaders.

This chapter will review the different professional disciplines to help you become knowledgeable about subtle but important differences between them. Then I will relate these to research I have conducted that shows how certain professionals evaluate the "top twenty" factors (presented in Chapter 8) differently than other professionals. Given this background on the professional disciplines, I will describe the kind of relationship you want to develop with any professional you recruit to be an ally—namely, a *consultation* relationship rather than a therapeutic or supervisory relationship. Finally, I will offer you practical guidelines as to how to locate, screen, and select your professional allies.

Attorneys

It is difficult to look in the yellow pages of a telephone directory and pick out an attorney—or any other kind of professional—who is tailor-made for your case.There are four methods that will help your selection efforts.

First, ask friends or relatives about attorneys they have used and from whom they have gotten good service. Even if attorneys they suggest do not handle child-custody cases, calling them, mentioning the friend who referred you, and asking for the name of a good child-custody lawyer is better than a random selection from the telephone book.

Second, most areas have a local bar association that will provide you with the names of lawyers who handle child-custody cases. The problem with the local bar association is that it is strictly a referral source and does not give you any idea about how good a lawyer may or may not be.

Third, if you have consulted other professionals, such as a psychiatrist or psychologist, or a social agency, you may be able to get direct information about the capabilities of a given lawyer (but professional ethics usually prevent complete candor).

Fourth, the public library or the library at a local college or university should contain a directory of the American Bar Association. In this volume you will find the listings for members of the Family Law Section. Members of the Family Law Section are known to have special expertise in domestic law, which includes child custody.

While it is still too early to assess, the recent U.S. Supreme Court ruling that it is appropriate for attorneys to advertise may open up a fifth method for selecting a lawyer. Assuming that bar associations establish stringent standards for "truth in advertising," it seems likely that the consumer will be able to gain some degree of evaluative information from the advertising of legal services.

Lawyers have completed three years of law school (usually after having spent four years earning a bachelor's degree). They receive a Juris Doctor degree. Most curricula for law schools are technically oriented, preparing the lawyer to maneuver the mechanisms of the legal system. Graduating from law school does not guarantee that the lawyer is knowledgeable about family law or child custody. In fact, family law (and child custody) is typically a very minor part of the law-school curriculum. Therefore, it is essential that your selection of a lawyer be based on investigating how much he or she really knows about child custody. Further, you should learn how much experience and success the lawyer has had with child custody.

With all professionals you are recruiting for allies, you should approach them on a one-time-only basis for mutual screening for compatibility. Since your attorney will be the primary consultant in your child-custody battle, it is particularly important that he or she demonstrate: knowledge of *current* child-custody statutes and practices; freedom from prejudice in favor of or against any factor that may be evaluated for you or your ex-spouse; an openness to using other professionals (such as psychiatrists, psychologists, or social workers) to strengthen your case; a willingness to involve you in the mapping of a battle plan; and above all, a respect for your human dignity. The lawyer's attitude toward you should enable you to find the relationship supportive in a healthy fashion and to be an equal (or even primary) partner in the planning and presentation of evaluative material. Use a one-time-only consultation session to evaluate the lawyer's potential in these areas.

In addition, your accepting an attorney or any other professional into your case should be prefaced by a clear understanding of mutual responsibilities. Preferably this understanding should be written out to create a contractual agreement. Financial reimbursement is, of course, a major factor that should be agreed upon from the onset. The agreement should specify both amount and payment arrangements.

Information on lawyers, including members of the Family Law Section, is available from the American Bar Association, 1155 East 60th Street, Chicago, Ill. 60637.

Psychiatrists

Psychiatrists are physicians. After receiving the Doctor of Medicine degree with appropriate supervised experience, they are required to spend an additional three years in a psychiatric residency, during which they receive supervised training in diagnosis and treatment. By virtue of their medical background, their treatment orientation tends to be more "drug-related." While their psychotherapy is essentially the same as that provided by professionals from other disciplines, such as psychology and social work, psychiatrists tend to combine such therapy with psychotropic drugs and other medications.

Psychiatrists are usually held in high public regard, and this elevated status can be a real advantage when they provide expert testimony in court. On the other hand, many medical specialists view psychiatry as one of the more ill-defined and "soft" areas of medicine, and among physicians it is frequently admitted that psychiatrists are less prestigious than more physically oriented specialists. Thus, other physicians might denigrate psychiatric testimony in court.

To assure maximum status, it is best to select a veteran practitioner—preferably one with many years of experience—with a Doctor of Medicine degree from a major university, important supervised experiences (such as having done a psychiatric residency in a renowned medical center), publications in professional journals, and, of major concern, the status of being a "Boarded" psychiatrist (a distinction accorded after specialty examinations by the American Board of Psychiatry and Neurology).

Beyond paper credentials, the psychiatrist—and this applies to all professionals to whom you might turn for consultation and/or expert testimony in the court proceedings—should have an impeccable reputation in the community in which the custody case will be heard. A professional surrounded in controversy or with an eccentric style is usually a liability, regardless of discipline. Further, the psychiatrist (and all other professionals) should be able to communicate effectively with you. Use your own instincts as the basis for evaluating this matter. For example, ask yourself if you come away from a conversation with the professional with a sense of having been listened to and respected and having learned from the exchange.

There is a potential liability to psychiatric testimony. As compared to behavioral scientists who rely on standardized assessment methods (such as psychological tests), the psychiatrist typically formulates his or her expert testimony around impressions created during an interview. While these opinions may be quite astute, they are, in fact, merely opinions and are highly subjective. In court, a standard procedure is to try to discredit the expert testimony introduced on behalf of the opponent. Thus, psychiatric testimony that is primarily opinion based on conversations is far less apt to stand up to cross-examination than opinions based on objective sources. This is why it is typically wise to involve more than one professional, such as both a psychiatrist and a psychologist, to bring in complementary supporting data.

The psychiatrist does have important recognition for involvement in child-custody legal proceedings, but care should be taken that his or her credentials are as outstanding as those of your ex-spouse's expert witness and that his or her views will not be devalued for lack of objectivity or facts.

Information on psychiatrists is available from the

American Psychiatric Association, 1700 Eighteenth Street, N.W., Washington, D.C., 20009.

Other Physicians

Most of the comments in the preceding section on psychiatrists can be applied to physicians representing other medical specialties. For child custody, a pediatrician, with specialized knowledge in child development, can be an important ally. A pediatrician should fulfill the standards cited for psychiatrists, such as extensive experience, impeccable community reputation, strong paper credentials, and so on. Pediatricians are "Boarded" by the American Board of Pediatrics. Testimony from a pediatrician contributing medical information and a psychologist contributing psychological test data can make a particularly strong combination. Similarly, family physicians or specialists from any medical area can bring high professional status into the proceedings on your behalf. For example, if your child has a special medical need, such as faulty vision or hearing or a physical handicap, specialists in ophthalmology or otology or orthopedics might be critical to your presenting an effective argument that you are best suited to meet the special needs of your child.

Information on physicans is available from the American Medical Association, 535 North Dearborn Street, Chicago, Ill. 60610.

Psychologists

Psychologists are behavioral scientists, not physicians. They usually hold a Doctor of Philosophy degree. Less frequently, they hold a Doctor of Education or a Doctor of Psychology degree. Psychologists have four or five years of graduate study (beyond a four-year bachelor's-degree program), including at least one year of supervised internship in the clinical application of behavioral-science principles of human development and behavior.

Be advised that there are psychologists of many ilks. In terms of specialties, there are experimental psychologists, physiological psychologists, industrial-organizational psychologists, educational psychologists, developmental-child psychologists, school psychologists, counseling psychologists, and clinical psychologists (among others). Unless there is some special issue, child-custody considerations would normally fall most in the realm of clinical psychology, but developmental-child psychologists, school psychologists, and counseling psychologists, depending upon their backgrounds, interests, and capabilities, can potentially make important contributions as well.

Like all professionals you select, the psychologist should present a strong community and professional image. Therefore, in screening a psychologist, you should inquire about the university awarding the degree, recognitions received from national professional organizations (such as being a Fellow of the American Psychological Association), publications in professional journals, training and employment records, and experience with issues related to child custody. In addition, you should determine whether the individual is licensed by the state board of examiners of psychologists in your state, and whether he or she is a Diplomate in Clinical Psychology under the auspices of the American Board of Professional Psychology.

This latter status is probably the highest credential possible for a psychologist, indicating that the professional has passed examinations to demonstrate clinical practice of a high quality. Diplomate status is available for the specialties of clinical, counseling, school, and industrial-organizational psychology.

Information on psychologists is available from the American Psychological Association, 1200 Seventeenth Street, N.W., Washington, D.C. 20036; and on Diplomates from the American Board of Professional Psychology, Suite 405, 2025 I Street, N.W., Washington, D.C. 20006.

Other Behavioral Scientists

Depending upon the issues unique to your child-custody situation, other behavioral scientists could be brought into the deliberations. Sociologists, criminal-justice specialists, criminologists, and others can contribute academically based evaluative material relevant to your suitability for custody.

Information on sociologists is available from the American Sociological Association, 1722 N Street, N.W., Washington, D.C. 20036; on criminal-justice specialists from the Academy of Criminal Justice Sciences, John Jay College of Criminal Justice, 444 West 56th Street, New York, N.Y. 10019; and on criminologists from the American Society of Criminologists, 1314 Kinnear Road, Columbus, Ohio 43212.

Social Workers

Social workers are typically trained in one of two broad specialties: social and organizational policy and planning; and social treatment. Obviously the first specialty would probably have minimal, if any, relevance to child custody, but the latter—social treatment—can be very important. Social treatment would encompass a foundation in human development and behavior and methods for evaluation and therapeutic treatment, all of which could be related to child and family factors.

Few social workers hold a doctoral degree. When they do, it is usually a Doctor of Social Work degree (which is primarily practice-oriented) or a Doctor of Philosophy degree (which is primarily research-oriented). A social worker with a doctoral degree would, logically, carry more status to expert testimony, all things being equal, than one with only the more common Master of Social Work degree (which requires two years of graduate study beyond the four-year bachelor's degree). In addition to all of the factors cited in previous sections as being important to all professionals, social workers should preferably hold ACSW status. Like the Boarded status for physicians and the Diplomate status for psychologists, certification by the Academy of Certified Social Workers reflects that the social worker has passed a practice-oriented examination and has professional credentials that are exceptionally strong. Since some states license social workers, licensing becomes another credential to look for.

Information on social workers is available from the National Association of Social Workers, 1425 H Street, N.W., Washington, D.C., 20005.

Marriage and Family Counselors

The terms "marriage counselor" and "family counselor" (and derivatives or combinations thereof) have only a vague meaning. Since few states have statutes to license or certify marriage and family counselors, it is not unusual for poorly qualified (and other self-ordained) persons to "hang out their shingle" as a counselor for marriage and family problems. Beware!

On the other hand, a legitimately trained marriage and family counselor can bring a high degree of expertise to child-custody issues. It is essential that you thoroughly investigate the qualifications of marriage and family counselors.

Since a marriage and family counselor is a generic classification (with few exceptions), professionals from psychiatry and other medical areas, psychology, social work, and education may be found under that title. But so too can religious leaders (which may or may not be appropriate for your needs) and lay persons. I know of one self-ordained "marriage counselor" in a state with no licensing law who did not finish high school, has no specialized training, and moves back and forth from "counseling" to selling real estate to some sort of mystical faith healing under a religious banner. While some people in our society might need that sort of person, it is certainly not in the best interests of you or your child to involve anyone other than the most highly qualified and solidly credentialed professional in the child-custody legal proceedings.

While it may be difficult to tell the good from the bad in the field of marriage counseling, one guideline might be to consider only those who hold "Clinical Membership" in the American Association of Marriage and Family Counselors. This Association has high standards for Clinical Membership, both in terms of academic preparation and supervised clinical practice.

Information on marriage and family counselors is available from the American Association of Marriage and Family Counselors, 225 Yale Avenue, Claremont, Calif. 91711.

Educators

The term "educator" masks about as many variations in expertise as the term "marriage counselor." Since contemporary child-custody statutes are specifying that educational factors be considered, there is a place for an educator with strong credentials and expertise directed at issues inherent to your unique case. Most commonly, a school psychologist, school counselor (or guidance specialist), or any number of child-development specialists employed in the schools would be the most logical for consultation. Credentials for educators vary greatly. A few may hold a doctoral degree, but most will hold a master's degree.

Probably the major considerations will be whether the educator has: employment in the schools in a leadership and/or highly responsible role; certification for the role (which is generally the case, or else the schools would not hire the person); an image among educators and in the community as a stable person and a respected educator; and documented expertise and experience with the specific factors that are under consideration in the custody determination.

Keep in mind that the higher the professional status (as witnessed by the job held), the better the community-professional image, the stronger the credentials, and the greater the experience possessed by the educator, the more effective will be his or her testimony. While this is true for all professionals, the nebulous term "educator" can best be evaluated by applying these standards.

Information about educators is available from the National Education Association, 1201 Sixteenth Street, N.W., Washington, D.C. 20036; about school counselors from the American Personnel and Guidance Association, 1607 New Hampshire Avenue, N.W., Washington, D.C. 20009; and about school psychologists from the American Psychological Association, 1200 Seventeenth Street, N.W., Washington, D.C. 20036.

Religious Leaders

"Religious leaders" include priests, ministers, rabbis, or any person associated directly with an organized religious organization. Such persons can be of benefit, but be sure that you do not rely too strongly on their image.

As mentioned in Chapters 7 and 8, religion has not often been considered of primary importance in child-custody cases. When religion has entered into the deliberations, it has been a factor in maintenance of continuity for the raising and development of the child.

Since there are often differing degrees of credibility attached to religious statements, it would seem best to minimize the role of religion in a child-custody case, except as it might be related to establishing your morality and value system and, if relevant, the continuity issue. Even then caution should be exercised.

Anyone speaking with religious zeal, even if it is compatible with your personal views, runs the risk of leading the court to consider, at the least, that the stance is too zealous to be credible or, at the worst, that the religion will jeopardize the welfare of the child.

If you involve a religious leader, seek one who has other attributes, such as a leadership role in the community, academic training in counseling or a related area, and communication skills that reflect moderation, persuasion, and eloquence.

Community Leaders

Most community leaders will probably not have formal qualifications as professionals, and so their testimony will generally be confined to statements about your character or the nature of your family (such as how they have observed you and your child getting along). What you are depending upon is that their community prominence will add value to their testimony. As with religious leaders, you should avoid community leaders who may have acceptance by only a limited segment of the populace (such as a political leader aligned only with a particular cause). You need rational testimony that will be accorded credibility by the court. In general, testimony from community leaders will have limited applicability and will usually be far less important than testimony from professionals.

Differences Between Professionals on the "Top Twenty" Factors for Mother Versus Father

I have commented several times about how personal bias can consciously or unconsciously creep into the views of even the most highly trained professional. In selecting an ally, it is essential that you assess the professional's ability to remain objective and open to evaluating factors that would serve your goal of winning custody.

I conducted a statistical analysis of the views expressed about the "top twenty" factors presented in Chapter 8 and have found that there were differences between professional disciplines and also between the sexes within those disciplines about how important a given factor was for a father versus a mother. The statistical analysis revealed that the professionals did consider some factors to be of greater importance for evaluating the father as opposed to the mother. And there were other factors that they considered to be of greater importance for evaluating the mother.

Of the "top twenty" factors, ten of them revealed significant differences between the professionals. I will present my research findings with the idea that in your selection of allies you should be especially sensitive to the fact that the categories of professionals I will mention for the ten factors considered the factor to be of greater importance for *one parent than for the other.* After presenting the evidence, I will point out how you can use these differences in importance for the benefit of you and your child and how you can guard against them in the event that your ex-spouse tries to capitalize on them.

I will present the ten factors in the same sequence that they appeared in the list in Chapter 8. This should allow you to read the section in this chapter, refer back to the appropriate section in Chapter 8, and create your own understanding about how this is relevant to the interests of you and your child.

PHYSICAL HEALTH: Female psychologists thought the mother's physical health was more important than that of the father.

GENERAL LIFE HISTORY: Male social workers thought the general life history was more important for the father than for the mother.

PERSONALITY: Female psychiatrists deemed personality more important for the mother than for the father.

MORALITY: Here there were some important differences. Morality was considered to be more important for the father by the female psychiatrists and the female social workers. On the contrary, male lawyers, female lawyers, and male psychiatrists thought morality to be more important for the mother than for the father.

CRIMINAL RECORD: Again there were differences. The father's criminal record was of greater importance in the eyes of the male lawyers, male psychiatrists, female psychologists, and female social workers, whereas the female psychiatrists thought the criminal record of the mother should be of greater importance.

INTELLIGENCE: The intelligence of the father was ranked of greater importance by the male psychiatrists and the female social workers, but the female psychiatrists ranked the mother's intelligence to be of greater importance.

KNOWLEDGE OF CHILD DEVELOPMENT: Differences are evident in the fact that knowledge of child development was considered to be of greater importance for the father by the male psychologists and female social workers, while it was of greater importance for the mother in the views of the female lawyers, male psychiatrists, and male social workers.

STABILITY OF RESIDENCE: Male lawyers thought stability of residence was of greater importance for the father, but male psychiatrists and male psychologists gave greater importance to this factor for the mother.

ASPIRATIONS: Aspirations were deemed of greater importance for the mother by the female lawyers, but for the father by the female psychiatrists.

SEXUAL BEHAVIOR: There were more differences for this factor than for any other one. The sexual behavior was thought to be of greater importance for evaluating the father by male lawyers, female lawyers, male psychiatrists, male psychologists, and female psychologists. In opposition, the male social workers thought that sexual behavior was of greater importance for the mother.

To explain the meaning of these findings, three things should be remembered. First, these findings come from a statistical analysis and say, in effect, that these categories or professionals assign greater importance to a factor for one parent than for the other and that probably they would operate that way in real-life cases. Second, there will be differences between professionals, so even if you sought a professional who was aligned in this research with supporting a certain preference, it is possible (but not probable) that his or her opinions would be different. And third, if a category of professional was not mentioned in one of the ten preceding paragraphs for one of the factors, it simply means that no statistical differences were discerned and that you will have to screen a little more closely.

As to how to apply these findings to your case, it is fairly simple. Whether you are relying on the differences cited here or whether you have learned through talking to your consultant that he or she considers a certain factor to be of greater importance for the father (if all else is equal) than for the mother—or vice versa—then you should capitalize on it if it will prove beneficial to your attack plan. But if it is clear that the professional's priorities are to your disadvantage—for example, if he or she expects higher standards of you than of your ex-spouse—then you should seek a different consultant or take steps to be sure that this priority does not enter into your case.

To exemplify the process, suppose that your ex-spouse had the established reputation of being sexually promiscuous during the marriage and leading a life style that could be characterized as "sexually liberated." If your ex-spouse were male, you might want to select a consultant from among male or female lawyers, male psychiatrists, and/or male or female psychiatrists on the grounds that they might tend to apply higher expectations to the sexual behavior of fathers than of mothers. On the contrary, if your ex-spouse were female, a similar thrust might best be gained from a consultant in the ranks of male social workers, since they (as a group) are known to place higher expectations on the sexual behavior of the mothers than of the fathers. It should be emphasized, however, that professional discipline alone does not preordain the stance of a consultant, so it is, at best, one of several factors for you to consider when selecting a consultant.

As you no doubt noticed, lawyers were mentioned for several of the factors as having significantly different values for the mother versus the father. Since you are so reliant on your lawyer, including for advice about what professionals to bring in for testimony, it is highly essential that you find out about the individual's priorities before you make a commitment to accept him or her as your legal counsel. Similar consideration should be exercised before agreeing to a certain attorney for your child's legal counsel, a decision which, in fact, might eventually be more critical than selecting your own attorney.

A Consultation Relationship

At several points, I have commented about the kind of relationship that you should try to establish with a professional, as well as on certain unhealthy aspects of a relationship that you should avoid, e.g., excessive dependency. In this section, I would like to sketch the basic ingredients of the preferred relationship between you and any professional you bring into the child-custody legal proceedings. Specifically, you should strive for a consultation relationship.

Of importance to child-custody determination, the consultant: should be able both to respect you and bring out the best in you (i.e., motivate you to contribute and do your best); should offer you information (through knowing what is important to custody determinations and evaluating your potential to fulfill the expectations of the court); should collaborate with you in planning your strategy; and should reinforce your functioning during the custody proceedings in a manner that will help you accomplish your objective—gaining custody of your child.

To summarize the functions in proper consultation, the consultant: helps you learn (usually by providing you with information and evaluative data); provides collaboration with mutual respect; shares responsibility for the outcome (but with emphasis upon your being honest and "healthy" in your efforts); and teaches or guides you toward presenting yourself to the court in the most favorable light.

The idea is twofold. First, a consultant can bring advanced academically based knowledge from his or her professional discipline to the court, in the form of expert testimony, that will aid you. Second, through the consultation processes, a consultant can help you establish a strong case for your suitability for meeting the best interests of your child.

Perhaps it can go without saying, but consultation is not therapy for you. You must not expect any consultant to eliminate your problems or arrange conditions after the custody determination to assure happiness for you and your child. Those are goals that only you can work for and eventually earn by restructuring your resources to be more effective in meeting the demands of living (more will be said on this matter in Chapter 11). Further, you must not adopt an attitude toward the consultant of

"Whatever you recommend is best." Rather, you must demand a collaborative relationship and be prepared to enter into the planning and presenting of your material as a strong, capable person. Beware of the consultant who tries to "take over" for you. This can only result in your being subservient to his or her value system, and contradicts the basis for the custody determination—that is, that you are able to be a responsible parent to your child.

Practical Guidelines for Selecting Professionals

Throughout this book and particularly in this and the previous three chapters, there have been many practical ideas about how to assess your suitability for child custody and how to involve professionals for sources of expert testimony. At this point, I would like to recapitulate some of the ideas in the form of offering you guidelines about how to select a professional for an ally in the custody battle. Consider the following guidelines:

1. Adopt a "consumer" posture, which means the professionals are to be in service to you (and your child) and you have a right to expect a quality performance from them.

2. Maintain the view that you are a capable and responsible person in the custody proceedings and that you will not allow yourself to be other than the central planner of the quest for gaining custody in order to meet the needs of your child.

3. Seek information about all possible professionals from authoritative sources (those who have no reason to guide you toward any one source) before making even the most tentative contact with the professional directly (family doctors, dentists, religious leaders, educators,

friends, family members, professional organizations, and so on can provide precontact information).

4. Use the ideas presented in the sections on the different disciplines in this chapter to do initial telephone inquiries and do not hesitate to ask for information about the professional's credentials in exact detail.

5. After narrowing the possibilities, apply the specific factors inherent to your custody case, such as the relevance of the "top twenty" factors to your situation, and the preferences of the professional disciplines, as presented in the section "Differences Between Professionals" in this chapter and the material in Chapters 7 and 8. Match these considerations to the characteristics of the remaining professionals on your list to select those with whom you want a "one-time-only"interview.

6. Move to select an attorney first, one with expertise in custody cases and with characteristics compatible with the ideas in Chapters 1, 8, and 9 and the section on attorneys in this chapter.

7. Select your attorney and establish a clear-cut agreement (perhaps even in written contractual form for the welfare of both of you) about mutual responsibilities.

8. Present your ideas about bringing in professionals for expert testimony to your attorney (do not hesitate to defend your beliefs), compare analysis of the importance of certain "top twenty" factors (be prepared to adjust your beliefs on the basis of your attorney's advisement and information), and construct and adopt a tentative strategy.

9. Having delineated the type of professional that can best contribute to your case, arrange a "one-time-only" interview, preferably in the company of your attorney (since your attorney must be able to work effectively with

the other professionals), but remain open to discounting the appropriateness of any potential professional, particularly if you detect that he or she might not be able to maintain objectivity or be optimally beneficial in expert testimony.

10. Select your professional consultants and enter in unreservedly with your attorney and professional consultants in an honest, open-minded, responsible, healthy fashion.

While these ten guidelines are but a skeleton of the procedure, review of the material in Chapters 6, 7, 8, and 9 and the preceding sections in this chapter should highlight the principles so that you can tailor your plan to your individual situation.

In selecting any consultant, you should keep in mind the statistical evidence that pointed out that professionals' personal factors (such as whether they are married and/or have children, their age, sex, and discipline, and so on) could lead to different priorities when evaluating a mother versus a father for suitability, and you should try to find the most highly statused professionals that you can afford. Consultants should be selected according to the factors that are relevant to your case and/or are known (by advice from your attorney) to be important in the mind of the judge who will be hearing the case. Naturally, such a decision about what professionals to involve depends, to a large extent, on what your ex-spouse is planning to do.

If your ex-spouse brings out the artillery, your firepower should be greater.

11.
The Reconstruction Period

DIVORCE is probably as psychologically brutal to a person as any other situation possible to encounter in life. When it also includes or is followed by a custody battle, the wounds are multiplied further. There is no doubt that psychological and even physical scars may be left. But after the ravages of any war comes the reconstruction period.

For the person who has experienced divorce and a custody battle, the period following becomes a time to try to get one's life back in order, maybe reconstructed to a condition as good as or better than before the war started. But there is a lesson to be learned from such war-torn countries as Germany and Japan: once the war has been waged, it is possible to learn from the experience, marshal new allies, and move into an era that promises a marked improvement over the past.

Facing this reconstruction is more than adopting a

"power of positive thinking" attitude, although a certain degree of positivism is needed to maximize chances of success. Just as divorce brings a new life style with ups and downs, gaining or losing the custody battle will usher in new problems that are very real and that must be countered with action.

Subsequent to divorce and/or custody disputes, it is common to have a period of mourning. Something has, indeed, been lost. Even if you won custody, there can be an awareness that day-to-day shared parenting for your children has now been permanently eliminated, and the loss can (and probably should) produce a feeling of regret.

As with any significant loss (such as death of a loved one), mourning for the loss of shared parenting should be kept in a realistic perspective. Granted, the loss may create less than ideal conditions for your child's development and life and you and your ex-spouse will not be able to share the rewards and responsibilities of parenting. Psychologically, this loss must be owned up to and accepted, and the mourning must not be allowed to continue on and on—to do so would be neurotic secondary gain.

The mourning may bring a sense of loss in life's meaning. In reality, this feeling may partially be based on a denial of the unhappiness that occurred in the marriage (which led to the divorce) in favor of an idealized fantasy about what could and should have been (which is obviously sheer fantasy or else the marriage would have flourished). The feeling may also stem from a reluctance to accept that one is responsible for salvaging and creating meaning in life without the support of a spouse.

There is no reason why the reconstruction period or life in the future need be less meaningful. In point of fact, there is reason to believe things can be more meaningful. It is well documented that second marriages seem to be better than the same persons' first marriages. The explanation for this improvement is simple: people learn from their errors and are prepared to work to ensure that the second marriage is rewarding.

The task facing the divorced parent is a confrontation with new types and degrees of responsibility, and the risk is of being overwhelmed by changes in life style and responsibilities. This is a critical phase, because there will be greater demands on time, resources, and ego strength for a single parent than for a two-parent team. Even the parent who failed to get custody may experience the demands as being greater. The stereotyped father without custody might find himself thinking, "Before I didn't mind working all the time because I knew my family was benefitting, but now I don't get to see the kids enjoying the fruits of my labor."

New responsibilities may include managing child care, finances, and social life. You will need someone to care for the children while you are at work, at the store getting a gallon of milk, taking the car to the garage to be serviced, taking one child to the doctor while the others are at home, and on and on—all the simple day-to-day tasks that are more easily handled by two people than by one. Finances will often be more difficult. Child-support payments may make it difficult or impossible to maintain the same standard of living, and you will either have to find a way to bring in more money on your own or adopt a more modest living arrangement. With or without custody, the end of "married living" will force you into a new image and role in society. Friends of many years will change their views about you and will want to have more or less contact with you because you are no longer married or because of your having or losing custody of the children. Social activities will be different, again because you are alone and have new responsibilities.

It is easy to sense why these changes in responsibilities and the concomitant changes in the sources from whom or from which you draw strength can be a heavy burden. They are real problems! Moreover, there is no simple answer.

Lest that seem overly bleak, I should hasten to add, however, that there are answers—just not a simple one. The answers lie, of course, in your setting about to reconstruct your existence.

A major step in the reconstruction is to integrate the total marriage and divorce experience, as well as all past experiences' into a new life structure. Early on, I mentioned that divorce did not end the relationship. At most, divorce signals the finale of the legally established marriage, but the relationship (or at least the impact of it) will continue on touching the lives of all involved—be it you, your ex-spouse, or your children. Consequently, you have not lost everything from your past marriage; you have gained a wealth of experiences. While accepting that the marriage is over—the divorce has finalized it—the years of marriage can and will continue on as influences, and your experiences with your ex-spouse equip you far better than before your marriage to find meaning from relationships, especially with the opposite sex. This point relates to the finding that second marriages are better than first marriages. The message, therefore, is to look on the past as a source of strength, which can justly arm you with confidence to encounter the present and the future.

Going beyond using the past to buttress your sense of confident readiness for the future, it is necessary to keep a clear head in order to plan and enter into a new life structure. Leaving a divorce and custody dispute behind necessitates avoiding the temptation to harbor unhealthy emotions and past memories. This point entails much more than simplistic advice, such as "Don't harbor a grudge" or "Let bygones be bygones."

It is normal to experience conflicting feelings, to grieve for the lost relationship(s) while striving to create new ones, and to feel that life's meaning has somehow diminished or escaped you. Ultimately, only you can accept and work through the conflicting impulses and feelings and move toward recognizing that you are, in fact, in a new stage of your life.

Obviously, negative feelings come and go and everyone experiences them, but they need not (and must not) be maintained and nurtured. Most important, the rational person does not translate them into self-destructive behaviors. If, however, you want to be self-destructive, it is your prerogative, but admit that you are the one making the destructive decision and do not inflict such an illogical decision on others (and as a parent, it is virtually impossible to adopt a self-destructive pattern without hurting others, namely your children).

With a mind-set free from unnecessary conflicts and with an acceptance of responsibility, you can move toward a new life structure. Most basically, it is necessary to delineate options for resolving the press of day-to-day problems. You may need to locate new child-care arrangements. Often this will necessitate changing your values. Many people say, "I would never leave my child with a stranger," but reality may dictate that a "stranger," in the form of a professional child-care agency or center or someone advertising in the local newspaper, will have to care for the child. Certainly, you would, of course, carefully scrutinize these individuals or agencies to be sure your child would be well cared for. You may also have to change your priorities in order to accommodate the children. For example, many single parents find it difficult to relinquish preferred activities (such as going to movies, playing tennis or golf, eating out, and so on) because there is no one to care for the children as before or because the budget can no longer support such activities. Finances may require that decisions about supplementing income or changing standards of living will have to be made within the context of reality, as opposed to personal preferences.

With the practical logistics of single parenting arranged, the next step is to accept that your new life structure is totally open for redefinition, that nothing is preordained as to how you should proceed into your life. You cannot justly blame others for holding you back, aside from what reality (such as child care or child support) imposes on you.

Psychotherapists with a rational approach to human behavior emphasize that there are certain irrational thoughts that serve no constructive purpose. At this redefinition point, people often find themselves inclined to engage in irrational thinking and to blame others and make them responsible for their own lack of happiness or lack of direction. It does not seem appropriate to go into a thorough analysis and explanation of self-defeating behaviors and how to be rational in your thoughts, feelings, and deeds, but I would refer to, among many possibilities, Albert Ellis' book *Humanistic Psychotherapy*. A major point of Ellis' work, and one that I apply with many of my psychotherapy clients, is that people are propagandized from birth by society, family, and friends to believe that things have to turn out a certain way, and when events or conditions turn out differently, a person may transform disappointment into a value judgment about his or her total worth, and say, in effect, "I'm no good."

For the single parent, with or without custody, the foregoing is crucial. To accept a propagandized outlook is virtually to eliminate the possibility of attaining a much-needed restructuring of the post-divorce life style.

Actually, there are very few things that others—society, family, friends—can prescribe as "right" for anyone else. Of course, we have laws that restrict our infringing upon the rights of others (and vice versa). But in terms of how we live our lives, that is strictly up to us and the value system that we, as individuals, choose to adopt.

Consequently, a situation that leads us to feel anxious, hostile, depressed, or guilty is not to blame. The cause rests in ourselves, and in the way we *think* about the situation. For example, the single parent who chooses to stay in his or her abode and wallow in depression because the ex-spouse received custody and to think that "now there is no way my kids will ever love me" has accepted an item of propaganda: "You are bad if you divorce, and if you aren't fit for custody there is no question about your being evil and unlovable." This kind of irrational thinking ignores the reality of living in our complex contemporary society; specifically, in this day and age of easy divorce and intense marital stress, being divorced and/or failing to receive custody does not mean "unfitness" *per se*. Society accepts that marriage may end if needs aren't met, and custody is based on which of the parents can *better* meet the interests of the child.

Finding an identity as a single parent is a major challenge. Even a bad marriage gives an identity. Our society provides ready-made accepted identity for any "married person." Stereotyping of this nature does not, of course, give any personalized identity, but it does provide some people—particularly those who are insecure and without much self-understanding and self-acceptance—with a superficial identity.

A personalized identity must be sought. Introspection can reveal the seeds for change. That is, deciding what is important to you, what your characteristics really are (as viewed by others as well as yourself), what you need in life, and what immediate options are open to you—these decisions can at least start you on the path to finding behavioral options that can promote a personal identity.

When this challenge is presented to single parents, it seems that the most common interpretation is, "You mean I need to find a new social life?" In part that is true, but it goes beyond the idea of seeking activities in a social context—it must be constructive, fulfilling involvement.

I offered a number of cautions about social activities and particularly sexual involvement in Chapter 7. As was probably evident, I believe that socialization holds more potential for reward than any other human function (aside from eating and other basic need-fulfilling acts for survival). But socialization also holds more potential for threat than any other human function as well.

The critical task for you during this reconstruction time is not to succumb to the seductive appeal of social contacts as a solution to all problems. At the same time, you should allow logic and your healthy needs to channel you into fulfilling relationships.

Self-analysis for purposes of better understanding what you are, what you need, and what you might be able to attain is always important. Because of the severe threat to self-worth and personal identity as a result of divorce and child-custody proceedings, it is vital that you devote effort to gaining greater insight and cultivating personal-psychological growth. This is the route to a new life structure. That is, effective insight leads to establishing values, fulfilling needs, and living a life style that represents an improvement over that of the past.

You may wish to seek professional help from a counselor or psychotherapist. If so, you should remember that the helper is just that: a helper. You are not in any way removed from responsibility for creating a better life for yourself. On the contrary, accepting a professional helper into the quest underscores your responsibility to make improvements.

Expectations for change should be reality-oriented. It took you a number of years to become what you are, and there is no reason to believe that you will make an overnight transformation—even with the best psychotherapist—into a totally new you. It will take time. It will take effort and much trial and error. And it will, in all likelihood, involve some additional defeats. Popular songs issue a reminder of reality: no one is promising you a rose garden!

Self-responsibility is one thing. Being responsible for others is quite another thing. It is difficult to internalize, but your responsibilities do not extend to guaranteeing an outcome for anyone else. This includes your family and friends—even your children.

Responsibility to loved ones (or for those you really care about, if "love" is too strong a word) means that you have a reciprocally beneficial relationship that requires, as part of it, that you give of yourself for the benefits of others. In turn, however, you should anticipate benefits. But of greater import, when others choose not to accept your giving or not to follow your preferred way, that in no way discredits you and you should not allow yourself to react negatively (such as by feeling guilty if someone disapproves of your behavior or by feeling that you should have done more to help if someone is unsuccessful in his or her life).

With your children, you do have duties, but you are not responsible for all of your children's behavior. This is especially true after they move toward the age of self-determination (i.e., adolescence).

In all of your relationships, you should strive to remain logical, consistent, supportive, caring, and reinforcing of positive conditions. Beyond these actions, you cannot assume responsibility for the outcome of relationships.

To make the reconstruction period a time for your greatest improvement ever, you must be prepared to be open-minded. You must allow past experiences and new learning to define and open doors to different behavioral options. This means experiencing situations differently than in the past. You must try to say things you would not have said before. You must allow yourself to feel in ways you never felt before. You must allow yourself to act in variation with the past. In other words, you must be prepared to be a "risk-taker."

You cannot predict the outcome of everything. But if you apply logical reasoning to your needs and options, rather than maintaining a simple rigidity aligned with the past, you should be able to cull through a myriad of behavioral alternatives—some of which will be positive and some of which will undoubtedly be negative. From this purposeful exploration of behavioral variety should emerge ideas about sources of reward that will promote personal growth and fulfillment.

Living carries no guarantees. Research on the stages of life reveals that we all eventually pass into a phase where we realize that "this is it—there ain't no more!" Then, if we're lucky, we can settle in and enjoy what life is all about: Being!

"Being" is a complex state of existence. There are no objective or factual cornerstones, save life itself. It is a process, a matter of continually trying to expand one's awareness of self and life. It requires being open to new inputs from others, but processing them according to your individualized systems. It is a commitment to develop, to create, to experience. It is striving for the "peak organism," a rich unification of mind and body unfettered by destructive feelings and maladaptive habits.

Our civilization has evolved from a series of wars. Humans have repeatedly fought "the war to end all wars." Ideally, your marital war would be your last. Realistically, it is probably just one of many that you will have to face at one time or another, although they may take forms such as unemployment, aging, debilitating illness, and death. But in between there can be refinement and meaning, perhaps in the forms of caring, love, marriage, sex, birth, parenting, creativity, productivity, and fun.

Appendix A

Top Twenty Factors for Mothers

1. Quality of relationship with the child
2. Mental health
3. Childrearing attitudes
4. Child-care history
5. Personal behavior
6. Physical health
7. Personality
8. General life history
9. Morality
10. Intelligence
11. Criminal record
12. Knowledge of child development
13. Income
14. Stability of residence
15. Aspirations
16. Education
17. Age
18. Sexual behavior
19. Religion
20. Vocation

Appendix B

Top Twenty Factors for Fathers

1 Quality of relationship with the child
2 Mental health
3 Childrearing attitudes
4 Personal behavior
5 Child-care history
6 Physical health
7 General life history
8 Personality
9 Morality
10 Intelligence
11 Criminal record
12 Income
13 Knowledge of child development
14 Education
15 Stability of residence
16 Aspirations
17 Sexual behavior
18 Age
19 Vocation
20 Religion

About the Author

Robert Henley Woody earned a Doctor of Philosophy degree in counseling psychology at the Michigan State University and a Doctor of Science degree in health-services research at the University of Pittsburgh. He was a Postdoctoral Fellow in Clinical Psychology at the University of London's Institute of Psychiatry and received a Postdoctoral Certificate in Group Psychotherapy from the Washington School of Psychiatry. He studied law at the Ohio State University's College of Law and the Thomas M. Cooley Law School. He has been in private practice as a psychologist, psychotherapist, and marriage and family counselor for almost two decades. In addition, he has been on the faculties at the State University of New York at Buffalo, the University of Maryland, the Grand Valley State Colleges, and the Ohio University, and is presently Dean for Graduate Studies and Research and Professor of Psychology at the University of Nebraska at Omaha.

Aside from this book, he has written five psychology textbooks and approximately 150 articles for professional journals. He is a Fellow of the American Psychological Association. He has been named a Diplomate in Clinical Psychology by the American Board of Professional Psychology, a Diplomate in Psychological (Experimental) Hypnosis by the American Board of Psychological Hypnosis, and a Certified Sex Therapist and Certified Sex Educator by the American Association of Sex Educators, Counselors, and Therapists. Beyond his work, Dr. Woody is a student of brass and fretted instruments and folk music.

References

ACKERMAN, N. W. *The Psychodynamics of Family Life: Diagnosis and Treatment of Family Relations.* New York: Basic Books, 1958.

CLARK, H. H., JR. *The Law of Domestic Relations in the United States.* Hornbook Series. St. Paul, Minn.: West, 1968.

Commissioners on Uniform State Laws. Uniform Child Custody Jurisdiction Act. *Family Law Quarterly*, 1969, 3, 317–30.

DESPERT, J. L. *Children of Divorce.* Garden City, N.Y.: Dolphin Books, 1962.

EDWARDS, A. L. *Manual: Edwards Personal Preference Schedule.* New York: Psychological Corp., 1957.

ELLIS, A. *Humanistic Psychotherapy: The Rational-Emotive Approach.* New York: McGraw-Hill, 1973.

FENICHEL, O. *The Psychoanalytic Theory of Neurosis.* New York: W. W. Norton, 1945.

FOSTER, H. H., JR., AND D. J. FREED. "A Bill of Rights for Children." *Family Law Quarterly*, 1972, 6, 343–75.

GARDNER, R. A. *The Parents Book About Divorce.* Garden City, N.Y.: Doubleday, 1977.

GOLDSTEIN, J., A. FREUD, AND A. J. SOLNIT. *Beyond the Best Interests of the Child*. New York: Free Press, 1973.

MARRIS, P. *Loss and Change*. Garden City, N.Y.: Anchor Books, 1975.

SLOVENKO, R. *Psychiatry and Law.* Boston: Little, Brown & Co., 1973.

TAVRIS, C., AND C. OFFIR, *The Longest War: Sex Differences in Perspective.* New York: Harcourt Brace Jovanovich, 1977.

WOODY, R. H. *Psychobehavioral Counseling and Therapy: Integrating Behavioral and Insight Techniques.* New York: Appleton-Century-Crofts, 1971.

——— "Sexism in Child Custody Decisions." *Personnel and Guidance Journal*, 1977, 56, 168–70.

WOODY, R. H., AND J. D. WOODY. *Sexual, Marital, and Familial Relations*. Springfield, Ill.: Charles C. Thomas, 1972.

Index

Abasement, as secondary need, 6–7
Absence, parental, 37–39
Academy of Certified Social Workers, 144
Academy of Criminal Justice Sciences, 143
Achievement, as secondary need, 5
Ackerman, Nathan, 39
Adultery, 76, 78–79. *See also* Morals of parents
Affiliation, as need, 6
Age of parent, custody and, 106–107
Aggression, as need, 7–8
Alcohol, tension and, 125
Allies, recruiting, 135–56
Alternative life styles, 85–86
American Association of Marriage and Family Counselors, 56, 108, 145
American Association of Sex Educators, Counselors, and Therapists, 108
American Bar Association, 137, 138
American Board of Pediatrics, 141
American Board of Professional Psychology, 142–43
American Board of Psychiatry and Neurology, 139
American Medical Association, 141
American Personnel and Guidance Association, 147
American Psychiatric Association, 141
American Psychological Association, 142–43, 147
American Society of Criminologists, 143
American Sociological Association, 143
Anxiety, neurosis and, 120–21
Aspirations of parents, 106, 150
Attorneys. *See* Lawyers
Autonomy, as need, 5–6

Behavior
personal, custody and, 97–98
social, custody and, 84–86

Index

Behavioral problems, 39–43, 124–25
"Being," 167
"Belated discharge," 122
"Best interests of the child" concept, 23–28, 59–61
  natural parents and, 74–75
  putative parents and, 87
Beyond the Best Interests of the Child (Goldstein, Freud, and Solnit), 24
Bias in experts, 61–67
"Bill of Rights for Children" (Foster and Freed), 22–23
Black's Law Dictionary, 71
Blackstone, William, 18

Catharsis, 122–23
Catholic Church, 108
Certified Sex Educators, 108
Certified Sex Therapists, 108
Change, as need, 7
Child-care history, 96
Child development
  basic principles of, 31–39
  parents' knowledge of, 47–48, 103–104, 150
Childrearing attitudes, 96–97
Children
  age of as factor, 65
  after divorce, 44–47
  divorce statistics and, 11–12
  illegitimate, 86–87
  impact of divorce on, 29–43
  legal rights, 2, 21–28
  quality of relationship with, 94–95
  stages of development, 31–39
  their preferences, 18–82
Children of Divorce (Despert), 40
Clinical Members, American Association of Marriage and Family Counselors, 56, 108, 145
Commissioners on Uniform State Laws, 25, 71
Common law, 73–74, 82–83, 90–91
Community leaders, as consultants, 148
Consultation relationship, 152–54
Contracts
  with lawyers, 138
  premarital religious, 84, 108
  separational, 86
Counselors, marriage/family. *See* Marriage/family counselors
Courts, 70
  jurisdiction, 69–73, 80–81
Criminal record, custody and, 101, 150
Criminologists, as consultants, 143
Custody
  defined, 14–16
  divided, 87–89
  history of, 16–18

Deference, as need, 5
Depression, 50, 113
"Desirable treatment," 75
Despert, J. Louise, 40
Diet, ego strength and, 124
Diplomates in Clinical Psychology, 142–43
Divided custody, 87–89
Divorce
  history of, 9–12
  parent-child relationship after, 44–47
  parents coping after, 47–56, 157–67
  psychosocial impact on children, 29–43
Dominance, as need, 6

Education of parents, custody and, 105–106
Educators, as consultants, 146–47
Edwards, Allen L., 5, 8
Ego, 118–20
  state, weakened, 117–19
  See also Ego strength

Index

Ego strength, 112–13, 115–29
  the body and, 124–27
  marriage and, 49–50
  professionals and, 129–32
Ellis, Albert, 162
Emotional problems, divorce and, 39–43, 119–23
Endurance, as need, 7
Exercise, ego strength and, 125–26
Exhibition, as need, 5
Experts. *See* Professionals

Family, government influence on, 16–20
Family counselors. *See* Marriage/family counselors
Family Law Section, 137–38
Fathers
  experts' views on, 93, 148–52
  history of custody and, 18, 23, 37
  morals and, 78–79
  status and, 79–80
  top twenty factors for (Appendix B), 169
Fenichel, Otto, 119–20
Feudal period, children during, 17–18
Financial resources, 79–80
Fitness test, 24, 126–27
Foster, Henry, 22–23
Foster parents, 16
Freed, Doris Jonas, 22–23
Freud, Anna, 24

Gardner, Richard A., 40
Geography, jurisdiction and, 70–73
"Getting distance," 122
Goldstein, Joseph, 24
Government and the family, 16–20
Grief reaction, 123

Handicapped
  children, 81–82
  parents, 99
Health of parents
  ego strength and, 124–27
  mental, 95–96
  physical, 98–99, 149
Heterosexuality, as need, 7
Homosexuals, custody and, 108
Humanistic Psychotherapy (Ellis), 162

Identification, children and, 36–37
Illegitimate children, 86–87
Income of parents, 79–80, 102–103
Insight, divorce stress and, 127–28
Intelligence of parents, 101–102, 150
Intraception, as need, 6

Judges, 68–74
Jurisdiction, 69–73, 80–81

Laws, state
  and awarding custody, 59–61
  and children's rights, 24–28
Lawyers
  for children, 27–28
  choosing, 136–38
  as consultants, 152, 155
Legal
  concepts and the family, 19–20
  rights for children, 2, 21–28
Life history of parents, 99, 149
Loss and Change (Marris), 123

Marriage/family counselors, 3, 9, 55–56
  as consultants, 144–45
Marris, Peter, 123
Maternal deprivation, 41–42
Mental health, 95–96
Mentally retarded
  children, 81
  parents, 102
Michigan Child Custody Act, 25–26, 104
Minnesota Multiphasic Personality Inventory, 100

Index

Morals of parents, 78–79, 100–101, 107–108, 149–50
Mothers
  assumed right to custody, 57–67, 77
  experts' views, 61–67, 93, 148–52
  history of custody, 18, 23, 37
  and morals, 78–79, 149–50
  and "successful party" concept, 76
  top twenty factors for (Appendix A), 168
Mourning period, 158
Murray, H. A., 8

National Association of Social Workers, 144
National Educational Association, 146
Natural parents, 74–76
Nebraska Supreme Court, 24–25
Need systems, 4–9, 129
Neurosis, traumatic. *See* Traumatic neurosis
"No-fault" divorce, 76
Nurturance, 34–36
  children and, 35–36
  as need, 7

Order, as need, 5

Parents
  contact after divorce, 44–45
  factors influencing custody, 92–110
  foster, 16
  impact of absence, 37–39
  legal rights to custody, 16–20, 24–26
  natural, 24–26, 74–76
  psychological, 24–25
  putative, 86–87
  single, 11, 158–67
  social behavior of, 84–86
Parents Book about Divorce, The (Gardner), 40
Pediatricians, as consultants, 141
Personal behavior of parents, 97–98
Personality
  custody and, 100, 149
  in marriage, 8–9
  secondary needs and, 4–8
  tests, 100
Physical health of parents, 98–99, 149
  ego strength and, 124–27
Physicians, as consultants, 141
Positive reinforcement, 114–16
Precedent cases. *See* Common law
Press, needs and, 8
Professional parents, custody and, 109–10
Professionals
  bias in, 61–67
  consultation relationship with, 152–54
  factors influencing, 91–110
  how to relate to, 129–32, 152–54
  mapping strategy and, 131–34
  practical guidelines to, 154–56
  recruiting, 135–56
Psychiatric problems, 40–43
Psychiatric treatment
  as custody factor, 95–96
  for divorced people, 55–56
Psychiatrists, as consultants, 139–41
Psychiatry and Law (Slovenko), 58
Psychoanalytic theory, divorce and, 119–23
Psychoanalytic Theory of Neurosis, The (Fenichel), 119–21
Psychobehavioral Counseling and Therapy (Woody), 115
Psychological parents, 24–25
Psychotherapy, 3
  for divorced people, 55–56, 125
  traumatic neurosis and, 121
Putative parents, 86–87

"Quieting-down" method, 122

Race, custody and, 82
Reconstruction period, 157–67

Index

Reinforcement, positive, 114–16
Religion
  custody and, 83–84, 108–109
  premarital contracts and, 84
Religious leaders, as consultants, 147
Residence, stability of, 104–105, 150
Retarded
  children, 81
  parents, 102
Rorschach Ink-Blots Method, 100

Same sex placement, 64–65
School counselors, as consultants, 146–47
Second marriages, 46, 159–60
Self-defeating behavior, 113, 116–17
Self-destructive behavior, 124–25, 161
Self-esteem, divorce and, 31, 42
Self-help, traumatic neurosis and, 122–28
Sex differences, 4, 58
Sex Educators, Certified, 108
Sexism
  custody and, 57–60, 77
  experts and, 62–67
"Sexism in Child Custody Decisions" (Woody), 62
Sex Therapists, Certified, 108
Sexual behavior
  as custody issue, 78–79, 107–108, 150
  post-divorce, 51–54
Sexual, Marital, and Familial Relations (Woody and Woody), 2, 56
Siblings, separating, 80
Single parents, 11, 158–67
Sixteen Personality Factors Test, 100
Sleep disturbances, 120–21
Slovenko, Ralph, 58
Social behavior, custody and, 84–86
Social relations, post-divorce, 116–17
Social workers, as consultants, 143–44
Sociologists, as consultants, 143
Solnit, Sidney J., 24
Stability of residence, 104–105, 150
Stanford-Binet Intelligence Scale, 102
Status
  of parents, 70–80, 102–103, 109–110
  of psychiatrists, 139
"Stormy" method, 122
Strategy, attitudes toward, 131–34
Succorance, as need, 6
Sullivan, Harry Stack, 8

Thematic Apperception Test, 100
Tranquilizers, 125
Traumatic neurosis, 119–23

Uniform Child Custody Jurisdiction Act, 25, 71
United States Bureau of the Census, 10–11

Visitation rights, 87–89
Vocation of parents, 109–110

Wechsler Adult Intelligence Scale, 102
Woody, Jane Davita, 56
Writ of *certiorari*, 70